COACHING YOUTH

SOCCER

SECOND EDITION

American Sport Education Program

Human Kinetics

Library of Congress Cataloging-in-Publication Data

Coaching youth soccer / American Sport Education Program. -- 2nd ed.
    p. cm.
    2nd ed. of: Rookie coaches soccer guide. c1991.
    ISBN 0-87322-831-6 (pbk.)
    1. Soccer for children--Coaching.   2. Soccer--Coaching.
  I. American Sport Education Program.   II. Rookie coaches soccer guide.
  GV943.8.C63   1995
  796.334'07'7--dc20   95-2206
                                                           CIP

ISBN: 0-87322-831-6

Coaching Youth Soccer is the second edition of *Rookie Coaches Soccer Guide*.

Acquisitions Editor: Jim Kestner; **Soccer Consultants:** Richard Logsdon, PhD and Jean-Claude de Raoulx; **Developmental Editor:** Jan Colarusso Seeley; **Assistant Editors:** Karen Bojda, Erin Cler, and Ed Giles; **Copyeditors:** Frances Purifoy and David Hamburg; **Proofreader:** Dawn Barker; **Typesetter and Layout Artist:** Francine Hamerski; **Text Designer:** Judy Henderson; **Cover Designer:** Stuart Cartwright; **Photographer (cover):** Photo Network/G. Hofstetter; **Interior Art:** Tim Stiles, cartoons; Tim Offenstein, line drawings; and Tom Janowski, Mac art; **Printer:** United Graphics

Printed in the United States of America   10 9 8 7 6 5 4 3 2

Human Kinetics
Web site: http://www.humankinetics.com

United States: Human Kinetics, P.O. Box 5076, Champaign, IL 61825-5076
1-800-747-4457

Canada: Human Kinetics, Box 24040, Windsor, ON N8Y 4Y9
1-800-465-7301 (in Canada only)

Europe: Human Kinetics, P.O. Box IW14, Leeds LS16 6TR, United Kingdom
(44) 1132 781708

Australia: Human Kinetics, 57A Price Avenue, Lower Mitcham,
South Australia 5062
(08) 277 1555

New Zealand: Human Kinetics, P.O. Box 105-231, Auckland 1
(09) 523 3462

Contents

Welcome to Coaching!

Coaching young people is an exciting way to be involved in sport. But it isn't easy. The untrained novice coach may be overwhelmed by the responsibilities involved in helping athletes through their early sport experiences. Preparing youngsters physically and mentally in their sport and providing them with a positive role model are among the difficult—but rewarding—tasks you will assume as a coach.

This book will help you meet the challenges and experience the rewards of coaching young athletes. We call it *Coaching Youth Soccer* because it is intended for coaches who are working with developing soccer players. In this book you'll learn how to apply general coaching principles and teach soccer rules, skills, and strategies successfully to kids. This book also serves as a text for the American Sport Education Program's (ASEP) Rookie Coaches Course.

We hope you will find coaching rewarding and that you will continue to learn more about coaching and your sport so that you can be the best possible coach for your young athletes.

If you would like more information about ASEP and its Rookie Coaches Course, please contact us at

ASEP
P.O. Box 5076
Champaign, IL 61825-5076
1-800-747-5698

Good Coaching!

Who, Me . . . a Coach?

If you are like most rookie coaches, you have probably been recruited from the ranks of concerned parents, sport enthusiasts, or community volunteers. And, like many rookie and veteran coaches, you probably have had little formal instruction on how to coach. But when the call went out for coaches to assist with the local youth soccer program, you answered because you like children and enjoy soccer, and perhaps because you want to be involved in a worthwhile community activity.

I Want to Help, but . . .

Your initial coaching assignment may be difficult. Like many volunteers, you may not know much about the sport you have agreed to coach or about how to work with children between the ages of 6 and 14. Relax, because *Coaching Youth Soccer* will help you find the answers to such common questions as these:

- What do I need to be a good coach?
- How can I best communicate with my players?
- How do I go about teaching sport skills?
- What can I do to promote safety?
- What should I do when someone is injured?
- What are the basic rules, skills, and strategies of soccer?
- What practice drills will improve my players' soccer skills?

Before answering these questions, let's take a look at what's involved in being a coach.

Am I a Parent or a Coach?

Many coaches are parents, but the two roles should not be confused. Unlike your role as a parent, as a coach you are responsible not only to yourself and your child, but also to the organization, all the players on the team (including your child), and their parents. Because of this additional responsibility, your behavior on the playing field will be different from your behavior at home, and your son or daughter may not understand why.

For example, imagine the confusion of a young boy who is the center of his parents' attention at home but is barely noticed by his father/coach in the sport setting. Or consider the mixed signals received by a young girl whose soccer skill is constantly evaluated by a mother/coach who otherwise rarely comments on her daughter's activities. You need to explain to your son or daughter your new responsibilities and how they will affect your relationship when coaching.

Take the following steps to avoid such problems in coaching your child:

- Ask your child if he or she wants you to coach the team.
- Explain why you wish to be involved with the team.
- Discuss how your interactions will change when you take on the role of coach at practice or games.

- Limit your coaching behavior to when you are in the coaching role.

- Avoid parenting during practice or game situations, to keep your role clear in your child's mind.

- Reaffirm your love for your child, irrespective of his or her performance on the soccer field.

What Are My Responsibilities as a Coach?

A coach assumes the responsibility of doing everything possible to ensure that the youngsters on his or her team will have an enjoyable and safe sporting experience while they learn sport skills.

Provide an Enjoyable Experience

Sport should be fun. Even if nothing else is accomplished, make certain your players have fun. Take the fun out of sport and you'll take the kids out of sport.

Children enter sport for a number of reasons (e.g., to meet and play with other children, to develop physically, and to learn skills), but their major objective is to have fun. Help them satisfy this goal by injecting humor and variety into your practices. Also, make games nonthreatening, festive experiences for your players. Such an approach will increase your players' desire to participate in the future, which should be the biggest goal of youth sport. Unit 2 will help you learn how to satisfy your players' yearning for fun and keep winning in perspective. And unit 3 will describe how you can effectively communicate this perspective to them.

Provide a Safe Experience

You are responsible for planning and teaching activities in such a way that the progression between activities minimizes risks (see units 4 and 5). Further, you must ensure that the field on which your team practices and plays and the equipment team members use are free of hazards. Finally, you need to protect yourself from any legal liability that might arise from your involvement as a coach. Unit 5 will help you take the appropriate precautions.

Provide Opportunities for Children With Disabilities

There's a possibility that a child with a disability of some kind will register for your team. Don't panic! Your youth sport administrator or a number of organizations (see Appendix C) can provide you with information to help you best meet this child's needs.

As a coach, you need to know about the Americans with Disabilities Act (ADA). Passed in 1990, the ADA gives individuals with disabilities the same legal protection that is provided for people of diverse race, gender, class, etc. The law does recognize that there are times when including an individual who is disabled might risk the safety of that individual and other players, but the exact way that courts are treating the ADA is still being decided. In general, the law requires that "reasonable accommodations" be made to include children with disabilities into organized sport programs. If a parent or child approaches you on the subject, and you aren't sure what to do, talk to the director in charge of your soccer program. If you make any decision on your own pertaining to the ADA, you may be vulnerable to a lawsuit.

Keep in mind that these children want to participate alongside their able-bodied peers. Give them the same support and encouragement that you give other athletes, and model their inclusion and acceptance for all your athletes.

Teach Basic Soccer Skills

In becoming a coach, you take on the role of educator. You must teach your players the fundamental skills and strategies necessary for success in their sport. That means that you need to "go to school."

If you don't know the basics of soccer now, you can learn them by reading the second half of this manual, units 6, 7, and 8. But even if you know soccer as a player, do you know how to teach it? This book will help you get started. There are also many valuable soccer books on the market. Two of the best references for beginning coaches of beginning players are *Coaching Soccer Effectively* by Christopher A. Hopper and Michael S. Davis and *Fun Games for Soccer* by Joseph Luxbacher. Both books are available from Human Kinetics by writing P.O. Box 5076, Champaign, IL 61825-5076, or by calling 1-800-747-4457.

You'll also find it easier to provide good educational experiences for your players if you plan your practices. Unit 4 of this manual provides some guidelines for the planning process.

Getting Help

Veteran coaches in your league are an especially good source of help for you. They have all experienced the same emotions and concerns you are facing, and their advice can be invaluable as you work through your first season.

You can get additional help by watching soccer coaches in practices and games, attending workshops, reading soccer publications, and studying instructional videos. In addition to the American Sport Education Program (ASEP), the following national organizations will assist you in obtaining more soccer coaching information:

American Youth Soccer Organization (AYSO)
5403 W. 138th Street
Hawthorne, CA 90250
(310) 643-6455

National Soccer Coaches Association of America
4220 Shawnee Mission Parkway
Suite 105B
Fairway, KS 66205
(800) 458-0678

Soccer Association for Youth (SAY Soccer)
4903 Vine Street, Suite 1
Cincinnati, OH 45217-1252
(513) 242-4263

U.S. Soccer Federation
U.S. Soccer House
1801-1811 South Prairie Avenue
Chicago, IL 60616
(312) 808-1300

U.S. Youth Soccer Association
A Division of the U.S. Soccer Federation
2050 North Plano Road, Suite 100
Richardson, TX 75082
(800) 4-SOCCER

Coaching soccer is a rewarding experience. And your players will be rewarded if you learn all you can about coaching so you can be the best soccer coach you can be.

Unit 2

What Tools Do I Need as a Coach?

Have you purchased the traditional coaching tools—things like whistles, coaching clothes, sport shoes, and a clipboard? They'll help you coach, but to be a successful coach you'll need five other tools that cannot be bought. These tools are available only through self-examination and hard work; they're easy to remember with the acronym COACH:

C—Comprehension

O—Outlook

A—Affection

C—Character

H—Humor

Comprehension

Comprehension of the rules, skills, and tactics of soccer is required. It is essential that you understand the basic elements of the sport. To assist you in learning about the game, the second half of this guide describes rules, skills, and tactics and suggests how to plan for the season and individual practices. In the soccer-specific section of this guide, you'll also find a variety of drills to use in developing soccer skills.

To improve your comprehension of soccer, take the following steps:

- Read the sport-specific section of this book.

- Consider reading other soccer coaching books, including *Coaching Soccer Effectively*, which is available from ASEP (see p. 142 to order). See other soccer resources on page 152.

- Contact any of the organizations listed on page 7.

- Attend soccer clinics.

- Talk with other, more experienced, coaches.

- Observe local college, high school, and youth soccer games.

- Watch soccer games on television.

In addition to having soccer knowledge, you must implement proper training and safety methods so your players can participate with little risk of injury. Even then, sport injuries will occur. And more often than not, you'll be the first person responding to your players' injuries, so be sure you understand the basic emergency care procedures described in unit 5. Also, read in that unit how to handle more serious sport injury situations.

Outlook

This coaching tool refers to your perspective and goals—what you are seeking as a coach. The most common coaching objectives are (a) to have fun, (b) to help players develop their physical, mental, and social skills, and (c) to win. Thus your *outlook* involves the priorities you set, your planning, and your vision for the future.

To work successfully with children in a sport setting, you must have your priorities in order. In just what order do you rank the importance of fun, development, and winning?

Answer the following questions to examine your objectives:

Of which situation would you be most proud?

    a. Knowing that each participant enjoyed playing soccer.

    b. Seeing that all players improved their soccer skills.

    c. Winning the league championship.

Which statement best reflects your thoughts about sport?

a. If it isn't fun, don't do it.
b. Everyone should learn something every day.
c. Sports aren't fun if you don't win.

How would you like your players to remember you?

a. As a coach who was fun to play for.
b. As a coach who provided a good base of fundamental skills.
c. As a coach who had a winning record.

Which would you most like to hear a parent of a child on your team say?

a. Billy really had a good time playing soccer this year.
b. Susie learned some important lessons playing soccer this year.
c. Jose played on the first-place soccer team this year.

Which of the following would be the most rewarding moment of your season?

a. Having your team wanting to continue playing, even after practice is over.
b. Seeing one of your players finally master the skill of dribbling without constantly looking at the ball.
c. Winning the league championship.

Look over your answers. If you most often selected "a" responses, then having fun is more important to you. A majority of "b" answers suggests that skill development is what attracts you to coaching. And if "c" was your most frequent response, winning is tops on your list of coaching priorities.

Most coaches say fun and development are more important, but when actually coaching, some coaches emphasize—indeed overemphasize—winning. You, too, will face situations that challenge you to keep winning in its proper perspective. During such moments, you'll have to choose between emphasizing your players' development or winning. If your priorities are in order, your players' well-being will take precedence over your team's win-loss record every time.

Take the following actions to better define your outlook:

1. Determine your priorities for the season.
2. Prepare for situations that challenge your priorities.
3. Set goals for yourself and your players that are consistent with those priorities.

4. Plan how you and your players can best attain those goals.

5. Review your goals frequently to be sure that you are staying on track.

It is particularly important for coaches to permit all young athletes to participate. Each youngster—male and female, small and tall, gifted and disabled—should have an opportunity to develop skills and have fun.

Remember that the challenge and joy of sport is experienced through striving to win, not through winning itself. Players who aren't allowed off the bench are denied the opportunity to strive to win. And herein lies the irony: Coaches who allow all of their players to participate and develop skills will—in the end—come out on top.

ASEP has a motto that will help you keep your outlook in the best interest of the kids on your team. It summarizes in four words all you need to remember when establishing your coaching priorities:

Athletes First,
Winning Second

This motto recognizes that striving to win is an important, even vital, part of sport. But it emphatically states that no efforts in striving to win should be made at the expense of the athletes' well-being, development, and enjoyment.

Affection

Affection is another vital tool you will want to have in your coaching kit: a genuine concern for the young people you coach. It involves having a love for children, a desire to share with them your love and knowledge of soccer, and the patience and understanding that allow each individual playing for you to grow from his or her involvement in sport.

Successful coaches have a real concern for the health and welfare of their players. They care that each child on the team has an enjoyable and successful experience. They recognize that there are similarities between young people's sport experiences and other activities in their lives, and they encourage their players to strive to learn from all their experiences, to become well-rounded individuals. These coaches have a strong desire to work with children and be involved in their growth. And they have the patience to work with those who are slower to learn or less capable of performing. If you have such qualities or are willing to work hard to develop them, then you have the affection necessary to coach young athletes.

There are many ways to demonstrate your affection and patience, including these:

- Make an effort to get to know each player on your team.
- Treat each player as an individual.
- Empathize with players trying to learn new and difficult sport skills.
- Treat players as you would like to be treated under similar circumstances.
- Be in control of your emotions.
- Show your enthusiasm for being involved with your team.
- Keep an upbeat and positive tone in all of your communications.

Some children appreciate a pat on the back or shoulder as a sign of your approval or affection. But be aware that not all players feel comfortable with being touched. When this is the case, you need to respect their wishes.

Character

Character is a word that adults use frequently in conversations about sport experiences and young people. If you haven't already, you may one day be asked to explain whether you think sport builds good character. What will you say?

The fact that you have decided to coach young soccer players probably means that you think participation in sport is important. But whether or not that participation develops character in your players depends as much on you as it does the sport itself. How can you build character in your players?

Youngsters learn by listening to what adults say. But they learn even more by watching the behavior of certain important individuals. As a coach, you are likely to be a significant figure in the lives of your players. Will you be a good role model?

Having good character means modeling appropriate behaviors for sport and life. That means more than just saying the right things. What you say and what you do must match. There is no place in coaching for the "Do as I say, not as I do" philosophy. Challenge, support, encourage, and reward every child, and your players will be more likely to accept, even celebrate, their differences. Be in control before, during, and after all games and practices. And don't be afraid to admit that you were wrong. No one is perfect!

Many of us have been coached by someone who believes that criticizing players is a good way to build character. In reality, this approach damages children's self-esteem and teaches them that their value as a person is based on how they perform in sport. Unit 3 will help you communicate with your players in a way that builds positive self-esteem and develops your athletes' skills.

Finally, take stock of your own attitudes about ethnic, gender, and other stereotypes. You are an individual coach, and it would be wrong for others to form beliefs about you based on their personal attitudes about coaches in general. Similarly, you need to avoid making comments that support stereotypes of others. Let your words and actions show your players that every individual matters, and you will be teaching them a valuable lesson about respecting and supporting individuals' differences.

Consider the following steps to being a good role model:

- Take stock of your strengths and weaknesses.
- Build on your strengths.
- Set goals for yourself to improve upon those areas you would not like to see mimicked.
- If you slip up, apologize to your team and to yourself. You'll do better next time.

Humor

Humor is an often-overlooked coaching tool. For our use it means having the ability to laugh at yourself and with your players during practices and games. Nothing helps balance the tone of a serious, skill-learning session like a chuckle or two. And a sense of humor puts in perspective the many mistakes your young players will make. So don't get upset over each miscue or respond negatively to erring players. Allow your players and yourself to enjoy the ups, and don't dwell on the downs.

Here are some tips for injecting humor into your practices:

- Make practices fun by including a variety of activities.
- Keep all players involved in drills and scrimmages.
- Consider laughter by your players a sign of enjoyment, not waning discipline.
- Smile!

Where Do You Stand?

To take stock of your "coaching tool kit," rank yourself on the three questions for each of the five coaching tools. Simply circle the number that best describes your current status on each item.

Not at all		Somewhat		Very much so
1	**2**	**3**	**4**	**5**

Comprehension _____

1. Could you explain the rules of soccer to other parents without studying for a long time?   1 2 3 4 5

2. Do you know how to organize and conduct safe soccer practices?   1 2 3 4 5

3. Do you know how to provide first aid for most common, minor sport injuries?   1 2 3 4 5

Comprehension Score: _____

Outlook

4. Do you place the interests of all children ahead of winning when you coach?   1 2 3 4 5
5. Do you plan for every meeting and practice?   1 2 3 4 5
6. Do you have a vision of what you want your players to be able to do by the end of the season?   1 2 3 4 5

Outlook Score: _____

Affection

7. Do you enjoy working with children?   1 2 3 4 5
8. Are you patient with youngsters learning new skills?   1 2 3 4 5
9. Are you able to show your players that you care?   1 2 3 4 5

Affection Score: _____

Character

10. Are your words and behaviors consistent with each other?   1 2 3 4 5
11. Are you a good model for your players?   1 2 3 4 5
12. Do you keep negative emotions under control before, during, and after matches?   1 2 3 4 5

Character Score: _____

Humor

13. Do you usually smile at your players?   1 2 3 4 5
14. Are your practices fun?   1 2 3 4 5
15. Are you able to laugh at your mistakes?   1 2 3 4 5

Humor Score: _____

If you scored 9 or less on any of the coaching tools, be sure to reread those sections carefully. And even if you scored 15 on each tool, don't be complacent. Keep learning! Then you'll be well-equipped with the tools you need to coach young athletes.

Unit 3

How Should I Communicate With My Players?

Now you know the tools needed to COACH: Comprehension, Outlook, Affection, Character, and Humor. These are essentials for effective coaching; without them, you'd have a difficult time getting started. But none of those tools will work if you don't know how to use them with your athletes—and this requires skillful communication. This unit examines what communication is and how you can become a more effective communicator-coach.

What's Involved in Communication?

Coaches often mistakenly believe that communication involves only instructing players to do something, but verbal commands are a very small part of the communication process. More than half of what is communicated is nonverbal. So remember when you are coaching: Actions speak louder than words.

Communication in its simplest form involves two people: a sender and a receiver. The sender transmits the message verbally, through facial expression, and possibly through body language. Once the message is sent, the receiver must assimilate it successfully. A receiver who fails to attend or listen will miss parts, if not all, of the message.

How Can I Send More Effective Messages?

Young athletes often have little understanding of the rules and skills of soccer and probably even less confidence in playing it. So they need accurate, understandable, and supportive messages to help them along. That's why your verbal and nonverbal messages are so important.

Verbal Messages

"Sticks and stones may break my bones, but words will never hurt me" isn't true. Spoken words can have a strong and long-lasting effect. And coaches' words are particularly influential because youngsters place great importance on what coaches say. Perhaps you, like many former youth sport participants, have a difficult time remembering much of anything you were told by your elementary school teachers but can still recall several specific things your coaches at that level said to you. Such is the lasting effect of a coach's comments to a player.

Whether you are correcting misbehavior, teaching a player how to kick the ball, or praising a player for good effort, there are a number of things you should consider when sending a message verbally. They include the following:

- *Be positive and honest.*
- *State it clearly and simply.*
- *Say it loud enough, and say it again.*
- *Be consistent.*

Be Positive and Honest

Nothing turns people off like hearing someone nag all the time, and young athletes react similarly to a coach who gripes constantly. Kids particularly need encouragement because they often doubt their ability to perform in sport. So look for and tell your players what they did well.

But don't cover up poor or incorrect play with rosy words of praise. Kids know all too well when they've erred, and no cheerfully expressed cliché can undo their mistakes. If you fail to acknowledge players' errors, your athletes will think you are a phony.

State It Clearly and Simply

Positive and honest messages are good, but only if expressed directly in words your players understand. "Beating around the bush" is ineffective and inefficient. And if you do ramble, your players will miss the point of your message and probably lose interest. Here are some tips for saying things clearly:

- Organize your thoughts before speaking to your athletes.
- Explain things thoroughly, but don't bore them with long-winded monologues.

- Use language your players can understand. However, avoid trying to be hip by using their age group's slang vocabulary.

COMPLIMENT SANDWICH

A good way to handle situations in which you have identified and must correct improper technique is to serve your players a "compliment sandwich":

1. Point out what the athlete did correctly.
2. Let the player know what was incorrect in the performance and instruct him or her how to correct it.
3. Encourage the player by reemphasizing what he or she did well.

Say It Loud Enough, and Say It Again

Talk to your team in a voice that all members can hear and interpret. A crisp, vigorous voice commands attention and respect; garbled and weak speech is tuned out. It's OK, in fact, appropriate, to soften your voice when speaking to a player individually about a personal problem. But most of the time your messages will be for all your players to hear, so make sure they can! An enthusiastic voice also motivates players and tells them you enjoy being their coach. A word of caution, however: Don't dominate the setting with a booming voice that distracts attention from players' performances.

Sometimes what you say, even if stated loud and clear, won't sink in the first time. This may be particularly true with young athletes hearing words they don't understand. To avoid boring repetition and yet still get your message across, say the same thing in a slightly different way. For instance, you might first tell your players, "Mark your opponent at a safe distance." Soon afterward, remind them to "Make sure the opponent you are guarding cannot dribble, pass, or shoot around you for an easy goal." The second form of the message may get through to players who missed it the first time around.

Be Consistent

People often say things in ways that imply a different message. For example, a touch of sarcasm added to the words "way to go" sends an entirely different message than the words themselves suggest. It is essential that you avoid sending such mixed messages. Keep the tone of your voice consistent with the words you use. And don't say something one day and contradict it the next; players will get their wires crossed.

Nonverbal Messages

Just as you should be consistent in the tone of voice and words you use, you should also keep your verbal and nonverbal messages consistent. An extreme example of failing to do this would be shaking your head, indicating disapproval, while at the same time telling a player "Nice try." Which is the player to believe, your gesture or your words?

Messages can be sent nonverbally in a number of ways. Facial expressions and body language are just two of the more obvious forms of nonverbal signals that can help you when you coach.

Facial Expressions

The look on a person's face is the quickest clue to what he or she thinks or feels. Your players know this, so they will study your face, looking for any sign that will tell them more than the words you say. Don't try to fool them by putting on a happy or blank "mask." They'll see through it, and you'll lose credibility.

Serious, stone-faced expressions are no help to kids who need cues as to how they are performing. They will just assume you're unhappy or disinterested. Don't be afraid to smile. A smile from a coach can give a great boost to an unsure young athlete. Plus, a smile lets your players know that you are happy coaching them. But don't overdo it, or your players won't be able to tell when you are genuinely pleased by something they've done or when you are just putting on a smiling face.

Body Language

What would your players think you were feeling if you came to practice slouched over, with head down and shoulders slumped? Tired? Bored? Unhappy? What would they think you were feeling if you watched them during a contest with your hands on your hips, your jaws clenched, and your face reddened? Upset with them? Disgusted at an official? Mad at a fan? Probably some or all of these things would enter your players' minds. And none of these impressions is the kind you want your players to have of you. That's why you should carry yourself in a pleasant, confident, and vigorous manner. Such a posture not only projects happiness with your coaching role but also provides a good example for your young players who may model your behavior.

Physical contact can also be a very important use of body language. A handshake, a pat on the head, an arm around the shoulder, or even a big hug are effective ways of showing approval, concern, affection, and joy to your players. Youngsters are especially in need of this type of nonverbal message. Keep within the obvious moral and legal limits, but don't be reluctant to touch your players and send a message that can only truly be expressed in that way.

How Can I Improve My Receiving Skills?

Now, let's examine the other half of the communication process—receiving messages. Too often people are very good senders and very poor receivers of messages. As a coach of young athletes, it is essential that you are able to fulfill both roles effectively.

The requirements for receiving messages are quite simple, but receiving skills are perhaps less satisfying and therefore underdeveloped compared to sending skills. People seem to naturally enjoy hearing themselves talk more than others. But if you are willing to read about the keys to receiving messages and to make a strong effort to use them with your players, you'll be surprised by what you've been missing.

Attention!

First, you must pay attention; you must want to hear what others have to communicate to you. That's not always easy when you're busy coaching and have many things competing for your attention. But in one-to-one or team meetings with players, you must really focus on what they are telling you, both verbally and nonverbally. You'll be amazed at the little signals you pick up. Not only will such focused attention help you catch every word your players say, but you'll also notice your players' moods and physical states, and you'll get an idea of your players' feelings toward you and other players on the team.

Listen CARE-FULLY

How we receive messages from others, perhaps more than anything else we do, demonstrates how much we care for the sender and what that person has to tell us. If you care little for your players or have little regard for what they have to say, it will show in how you attend and listen to them. Check yourself. Do you find your mind wandering to what you are going to do after practice while one of your players is talking to you? Do you frequently have to ask your players, "What did you say?" If so, you need to work on your receiving mechanics of attending and listening. But perhaps the most critical question you should ask yourself, if you find that you're missing the messages your players send, is this: Do I care?

How Do I Put It All Together?

So far we've discussed separately the sending and receiving of messages. But we all know that senders and receivers switch roles several times during an interaction. One person initiates a communication by sending a message to another person, who then receives the message. The receiver then switches roles and becomes the sender by responding to the person who sent the initial message. These verbal and nonverbal responses are called feedback.

Your players will be looking to you for feedback all the time. They will want to know how you think they are performing, what you think of their ideas, and whether their efforts please you. Obviously, you can respond in many different ways. How you respond will strongly affect your players. So let's take a look at a few general types of feedback and examine their possible effects.

Providing Instructions

With young players, much of your feedback will involve answering questions about how to play soccer. Your instructive responses to these questions should include both verbal and nonverbal feedback. Here are some suggestions for giving instructional feedback:

- Keep verbal instructions simple and concise.

- Use demonstrations to provide nonverbal instructional feedback (see unit 4).

- "Walk" players through the skill, or use a slow-motion demonstration if they are having trouble learning.

Correcting Errors

When your players perform incorrectly, you need to provide informative feedback to correct the error—and the sooner the better. And when you do correct errors, keep in mind these two principles: Use negative criticism sparingly, and keep calm.

Use Negative Criticism Sparingly

Although you may need to punish players for horseplay or dangerous activities by scolding or removing them from activity temporarily, avoid reprimanding players for performance errors. Admonishing players for honest mistakes makes them afraid to even try. Nothing ruins a youngster's enjoyment of a sport more than a coach who harps on every miscue. So instead, correct your players by using the positive approach. Your players will enjoy playing more, and you'll enjoy coaching more.

Keep Calm

Don't fly off the handle when your players make mistakes. Remember, you're coaching young and inexperienced players, not pros. You'll therefore see more incorrect than correct technique, and you'll probably have more discipline problems than you expect. But throwing a tantrum over each error or misbehavior will only inhibit your players or suggest to them the wrong kind of behavior to model. So let your players know that mistakes aren't the end of the world; stay cool!

Positive Feedback

Praising players when they have performed or behaved well is an effective way of getting them to repeat (or try to repeat) that behavior in the future. And positive feedback for effort is an especially effective way to motivate youngsters to work on difficult skills. So rather than shouting and providing negative feedback to a player who has made a mistake, try offering players a "compliment sandwich," described on page 22.

Sometimes just the way you word feedback can make it more positive than negative. For example, instead of saying, "Don't shoot the ball that way," you might say, "Shoot the ball this way."

Then your players will be focusing on what to do instead of what not to do.

You can give positive feedback verbally and nonverbally. Telling a player, especially in front of teammates, that he or she has performed well, is a great way to boost the confidence of a youngster. And a pat on the back or a handshake can be a very tangible way of communicating your recognition of a player's performance.

Coaches, be positive!

Only a very small percentage of ASEP-trained coaches' behaviors are negative.

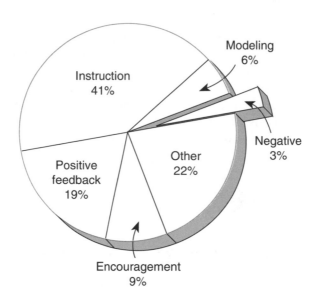

Who Else Do I Need to Communicate With?

Coaching involves not only sending and receiving messages and providing proper feedback to players, but also interacting with parents, fans, game officials, and opposing coaches. If you don't communicate effectively with these groups of people, your coaching career will be unpleasant and short-lived. So try the following suggestions for communicating with these groups.

Parents

A player's parents need to be assured that their son or daughter is under the direction of a coach who is both knowledgeable about the sport and concerned about the youngster's well-being. You can put their worries to rest by holding a preseason parent orientation meeting in which you describe your background and your approach to coaching.

If parents contact you with a concern during the season, listen to them closely and try to offer positive responses. If you need to communicate with parents, catch them after a practice, give them a phone call, or send a note through the mail. Messages sent to parents through children are too often lost, misinterpreted, or forgotten.

Fans

The stands probably won't be overflowing at your games, but that only means that you'll more easily hear the few fans who criticize your coaching. When you hear something negative said about the job you're doing, don't respond. Keep calm, consider whether the message had any value, and if not, forget it. Acknowledging critical, unwarranted comments from a fan during a contest will only encourage others to voice their opinions. So put away your "rabbit ears" and communicate to fans, through your actions, that you are a confident, competent coach.

Prepare your players for fans' criticisms. Tell them it is you, not the spectators, to whom they should listen. If you notice that one of your players is rattled by a fan's comment, reassure the player that your evaluation is more objective and favorable—and the one that counts.

Game Officials

How you communicate with officials will have a great influence on the way your players behave toward them. Therefore you need to set an example. Greet officials with a handshake, an introduction, and perhaps some casual conversation about the upcoming contest. Indicate your respect for them before, during, and after the contest. Don't make nasty remarks, shout, or use disrespectful body gestures. Your players will see you do it, and they'll get the idea that such behavior is appropriate. Plus, if the official hears or sees you, the communication between the two of you will break down.

Opposing Coaches

Make an effort to visit with the coach of the opposing team before the game. Perhaps the two of you can work out a special arrangement for the contest, such as free substitution of players. During the game, don't get into a personal feud with the opposing coach. Remember, it's the kids, not the coaches, who are competing. And by getting along well with the opposing coach, you'll show your players that competition involves cooperation.

✔ Summary Checklist

Now, check your coach-communication skills by answering "Yes" or "No" to the following questions.

		Yes	No
1.	Are your verbal messages to your players positive and honest?	____	____
2.	Do you speak loudly, clearly, and in a language your athletes understand?	____	____
3.	Do you remember to repeat instructions to your players, in case they didn't hear you the first time?	____	____
4.	Are the tone of your voice and your nonverbal messages consistent with the words you use?	____	____
5.	Do your facial expressions and body language express interest in and happiness with your coaching role?	____	____
6.	Are you attentive to your players and able to pick up even their small verbal and nonverbal cues?	____	____
7.	Do you really care about what your athletes say to you?	____	____
8.	Do you instruct rather than criticize when your players make errors?	____	____
9.	Are you usually positive when responding to things your athletes say and do?	____	____
10.	Do you try to communicate in a cooperative and respectful manner with players' parents, fans, game officials, and opposing coaches?	____	____

If you answered "No" to any of the above questions, you may want to refer back to the section of the chapter where the topic was discussed. Now is the time to address communication problems, not when you're coaching young athletes.

Unit 4

How Do I Get My Team Ready to Play?

To coach soccer, you must understand the basic rules, skills, and strategies of the sport. The second part of this book provides the basic information you'll need to comprehend the sport.

But all the soccer knowledge in the world will do you little good unless you present it effectively to your players. That's why this unit is so important. Here you will learn the steps to take when teaching sport skills, as well as practical guidelines for planning your season and individual practices.

How Do I Teach Sport Skills?

Many people believe that the only qualification needed to coach is to have played the sport. It's helpful to have played, but there is much more to coaching successfully. And even if you haven't played or even watched soccer, you can still learn to coach successfully with this IDEA:

> I—Introduce the skill.
>
> D—Demonstrate the skill.
>
> E—Explain the skill.
>
> A—Attend to players practicing the skill.

Introduce the Skill

Players, especially young and inexperienced ones, need to know what skill they are learning and why they are learning it. You should therefore take these three steps every time you introduce a skill to your players:

1. Get your players' attention.
2. Name the skill.
3. Explain the importance of the skill.

Get Your Players' Attention

Because youngsters are easily distracted, use some method to get their attention. Some coaches use interesting news items or stories. Others use jokes. And others simply project enthusiasm that gets their players to listen. Whatever method you use, speak slightly above the normal volume and look your players in the eye when you speak.

Also, position players so they can see and hear you. Arrange the players in two or three evenly spaced rows, facing you and not the sun or some source of distraction. Then ask if all can see you before you begin.

Name the Skill

Although you might mention other common names for the skill, decide which one you'll use and stick with it. This will help avoid confusion and enhance communication among your players.

Explain the Importance of the Skill

Although the importance of a skill may be apparent to you, your players may be less able to see how the skill will help them become better soccer players. Offer them a reason for learning the skill and describe how the skill relates to more advanced skills.

> *"The most difficult aspect of coaching is this: Coaches must learn to let athletes learn. Sport skills should be taught so they have meaning to the child, not just meaning to the coach."*
>
> Rainer Martens, ASEP Founder

Demonstrate the Skill

The demonstration step is the most important part of teaching sport skills to young players who may have never done anything closely resembling the skill. They need a picture, not just words. They need to see how the skill is performed.

If you are unable to perform the skill correctly, have an assistant coach, one of your players, or someone skilled in soccer perform the demonstration. These tips will help make your demonstrations more effective:

- Use correct form.
- Demonstrate the skill several times.
- Slow down the action, if possible, during one or two performances so players can see every movement involved in the skill.
- Perform the skill at different angles so your players can get a full perspective of it.
- Demonstrate the skill with both the right and the left legs.

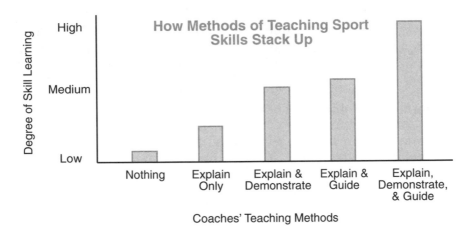

Explain the Skill

Players learn more effectively when they're given a brief explanation of the skill along with the demonstration. Use simple terms and, if possible, relate the skill to previously learned skills. Ask your players whether they understand your description. A good technique is to ask the team to repeat your explanation. Ask questions like "What are you going to do first?" "Then what?" Watch for looks of confusion or uncertainty and repeat your explanation and demonstration of those points. If possible, use different words so that your players get a chance to try to understand from a different perspective.

Complex skills often are better understood when they are explained in more manageable parts. For instance, if you want to teach your players how to change direction when they dribble the ball, you might take the following steps:

1. Show them a correct performance of the entire skill, and explain its function in soccer.

2. Break down the skill and point out its component parts to your players.

3. Have players perform each of the component skills you have already taught them, such as dribbling while running, changing speed, and changing direction.

4. After players have demonstrated their ability to perform the separate parts of the skill in sequence, reexplain the entire skill.

5. Have players practice the skill.

One caution: Young players have short attention spans, and a long demonstration or explanation of the skill will bore them. So spend no more than a few minutes combined on the introduction, demonstration, and explanation phases. Then get the players active in attempts to perform the skill. The total IDEA should be completed in 10 minutes or less, followed by individual and group practice activities.

Attend to Players Practicing the Skill

If the skill you selected was within your players' capabilities, and you have done an effective job of introducing, demonstrating, and explaining it, your players should be ready to attempt the skill. Some players may need to be physically guided through the movements during their first few attempts. Walking unsure athletes through the skill in this way will help them gain confidence to perform the skill on their own.

Your teaching duties don't end when all your athletes have demonstrated that they understand how to perform the skill. In fact, a significant part of your teaching will involve observing closely the hit-and-miss trial performances of your players.

As you observe players' efforts in drills and activities, offer positive, corrective feedback in the form of the "compliment sandwich" described in unit 3. If a player performs the skill properly, acknowledge it and offer praise. Keep in mind that your feedback will have a great influence on your players' motivation to practice and improve their performance.

Remember, too, that young players need individual instruction. So set aside a time before, during, or after practice to give individual help.

What Planning Do I Need to Do?

Beginning coaches often make the mistake of showing up for the first practice with no particular plan in mind. These coaches find that their practices are unorganized, their players are frustrated and inattentive, and the amount and quality of their skill instruction is limited. Planning is essential to successful teaching and coaching. And it doesn't begin on the way to practice!

Preseason Planning

Effective coaches begin planning well before the start of the season. Among the preseason measures that will make the season more enjoyable, successful, and safe for you and your players are the following:

- Familiarize yourself with the sport organization you are involved in, especially its philosophy and goals regarding youth sport.
- Examine the availability of facilities, equipment, instructional aids, and other materials needed for practices and games.
- Find out what fund-raising you and your players will be expected to do, and decide on the best way to meet your goals.
- Make arrangements for any team travel that will be required during the season. Consider clearance forms, supervision, transportation, equipment, contacting parents, and safety.

- Check to see whether you have adequate liability insurance to cover you when one of your players is hurt (see unit 5). If you don't, get some.
- Establish your coaching priorities regarding having fun, developing players' skills, and winning.
- Select and meet with your assistant coaches to discuss the philosophy, goals, team rules, and plans for the season.

- Register players for the team. Have them complete a player information form and obtain medical clearance forms, if required.

- Institute an injury-prevention program for your players.

- Hold an orientation meeting to inform parents of your background, philosophy, goals, and instructional approach. Also, give a brief overview of soccer rules, terms, and strategies to familiarize parents or guardians with the sport.

You may be surprised at the number of things you should do even before the first practice. But if you address them during the preseason, the season will be much more enjoyable and productive for you and your players.

In-Season Planning

Your choice of activities during the season should be based on whether they will help your players develop physical and mental skills, knowledge of rules and game tactics, sportsmanship, and love for the sport. All of these goals are important, but we'll focus on the skills and tactics of soccer to give you an idea of how to itemize your objectives.

Goal Setting

What you plan to do during the season must be reasonable for the maturity and skill level of your players. In terms of soccer skills and tactics, you should teach young players the basics and move on to more complex activities only after the players have mastered these easier techniques and strategies.

To begin the season, your instructional goals might include the following:

- Players will be able to pass by using the inside, outside, and top of the foot.
- Players will be able to trap by using the cushioning method of control.
- Players will be able to dribble under control, keep the ball close to their feet, and use moves and fakes to dribble past opposing players.
- Players will be able to head the ball forward while keeping their feet on the ground.
- Players will be able to shoot on goal with either foot.
- Players will be able to play goalkeeper and block shots on the ground and in the air.
- Players will be able to perform a throw-in, goal kick, corner kick, and free kick.
- Players will demonstrate knowledge of soccer rules.
- Players will demonstrate knowledge of basic offensive and defensive strategies.

Organizing

After you've defined the skills and tactics you want your players to learn during the season, you can plan how to teach them to your players in practices. But be flexible! If your players are having difficulty learning a skill or tactic, take some extra time until they get the hang of it—even if that means moving back your schedule. After all, if your players are unable to perform the fundamental skills, they'll never execute the more complex skills you have scheduled for them, and they won't have much fun trying.

Still, it helps to have a plan for progressing players through skills during the season. The 4-week sample of a season plan in Appendix A shows how to schedule your skill instruction in an organized and progressive manner. If this is your first coaching experience, you may wish to follow the plan as it stands. If you have some previous experience, you may want to modify the schedule to better fit the needs of your team.

The way you organize your season may also help your players to develop socially and psychologically. By giving your players responsibility for certain aspects of practices—leading warm-up and stretching activities are common examples—you help players to develop self-esteem and take responsibility for themselves and the team. As you plan your season, consider ways to provide your players with experiences that lead them to steadily improve these skills.

What Makes Up a Good Practice?

A good instructional plan makes practice preparation much easier. Have players work on more important and less difficult goals in early-season practice sessions. And see to it that players master basic skills before moving on to more advanced ones.

It is helpful to establish one goal for each practice; but try to include a variety of activities related to that goal. For example, although your primary objective might be to improve players' dribbling skill, you should have players perform several different drills designed to enhance that single skill. To add more variety to your practices, vary the order of the activities.

In general, we recommend that in each of your practices you do the following:

- *Warm up.*
- *Practice previously taught skills.*
- *Teach and practice new skills.*
- *Practice under match-like conditions.*
- *Cool down.*
- *Evaluate.*

Warm Up

As you're checking the roster and announcing the performance goals for the practice, your players should be preparing their bodies for vigorous activity. A 5- to 10-minute period of easy-paced activities, stretching, and calisthenics should be sufficient for youngsters to limber their muscles and reduce the risk of injury.

Practice Previously Taught Skills

Devote part of each practice to having players work on the fundamental skills they already know. But remember, kids like variety. Thus you should organize and modify drills so that everyone is involved and stays interested. Praise and encourage players when you notice improvement, and offer individual assistance to those who need help.

Teach and Practice New Skills

Gradually build on your players' existing skills by giving players something new to practice each session. The proper method for teaching sport skills is described on pages 36–40. Refer to those pages if you have any questions about teaching new skills or if you want to evaluate your teaching approach periodically during the season.

Practice Under Match-Like Conditions

Competition among teammates during practices prepares players for actual matches and informs young athletes about their abilities relative to their peers. Youngsters also seem to have more fun in competitive activities.

You can create match-like conditions by using competitive drills, modified games, and scrimmages (see units 7 and 8). However, consider the following guidelines before introducing competition into your practices:

- All players should have an equal opportunity to participate.
- Match players by ability and physical maturity.
- Make sure that players can execute fundamental skills before they compete in groups.
- Emphasize performing well, not winning, in every competition.
- Give players room to make mistakes by avoiding constant evaluation of their performances.

Cool Down

Each practice should wind down with a 5- to 10-minute period of light exercise, including jogging, performance of simple skills, and some stretching. The cool-down allows athletes' bodies to return to the resting state and avoid stiffness, and it affords you an opportunity to review the practice.

Evaluate

At the end of practice spend a few minutes with your players reviewing how well the session accomplished the goals you had set. Even if your evaluation is negative, show optimism for future practices and send players off on an upbeat note.

How Do I Put a Practice Together?

Simply knowing the six practice components is not enough. You must also be able to arrange those components into a logical progression and fit them into a time schedule. Now, using your instructional goals as a guide for selecting what skills to have your players work on, try to plan several soccer practices you might conduct. The following example should help you get started.

Sample Practice Plan

Performance Objective. Players will be able to complete a short pass with the inside of the foot.

Component	Time	Activity or drill
Warm up	10 min	Dribble around the field Calisthenics
Practice	20 min	Circle pass Take a walk
Teach	10 min	Short passing with inside of the foot Passing with a partner (both feet)
Scrimmage	15 min	Small-sided scrimmage
Cool down and evaluate	10 min	Easy jogging Stretching

✔ *Summary Checklist*

During your soccer season, check your planning and teaching skills periodically. As you gain more coaching experience, you should be able to answer yes to each of the following.

When you plan, do you remember to plan for

_____ preseason events such as player registration, fund-raising, travel, liability protection, use of facilities, and parent orientation?

_____ season goals such as the development of players' physical skills, mental skills, sportsmanship, and enjoyment?

_____ practice components such as warm-up, practicing previously taught skills, teaching and practicing new skills, practicing under match-like conditions, cool-down, and evaluation?

When you teach sport skills to your players, do you

_____ arrange the players so all can see and hear?

_____ introduce the skill clearly and explain its importance?

_____ demonstrate the skill properly several times?

_____ explain the skill simply and accurately?

_____ attend closely to players practicing the skill?

_____ offer corrective, positive feedback or praise after observing players' attempts at the skill?

What About Safety?

One of your players appears to break free down the field, dribbling the ball. But a defender catches up with, and accidentally trips, the goal-bound player. You notice that your player is not getting up from the ground and seems to be in pain. What do you do?

No coach wants to see players get hurt. But injury remains a reality of sport participation; consequently, you must be prepared to provide first aid when injuries occur and to protect yourself against unjustified lawsuits. Fortunately, there are many preventive measures coaches can institute to reduce the risk. This unit will describe how you can

- create the safest possible environment for your players,
- provide emergency first aid to players when they get hurt, and
- protect yourself from injury liability.

How Do I Keep My Players From Getting Hurt?

Injuries may occur because of poor preventive measures. Part of your planning, described in unit 4, should include steps that give your players the best possible chance for injury-free participation. These steps include the following:

- *Preseason physical examination*
- *Nutrition*
- *Physical conditioning*
- *Equipment and facilities inspection*
- *Matching athletes by physical maturity, and warning of inherent risks*
- *Proper supervision and record keeping*
- *Providing water breaks*
- *Warm-up and cool-down*

Preseason Physical Examination

In the absence of severe injury or ongoing illness, your players should have a physical examination every 2 years. If a player has a known complication, a physician's consent should be obtained before participation is allowed. You should also have players' parents or guardians sign a participation agreement form and a release form to allow their children to be treated in the case of an emergency.

Nutrition

Increasingly, disordered eating and unhealthy dietary habits are encroaching on youth soccer players. Let players and parents know the importance of healthy eating and the dangers that can arise from efforts to lose weight too quickly. Young soccer players need to supply their bodies with the extra energy they need to keep up with the demands of practices and matches. Ask your director about information that you can pass on to your players and their parents, and include a discussion of basic, commonsense nutrition in your parent orientation meeting.

Physical Conditioning

Muscles, tendons, and ligaments unaccustomed to vigorous and long-lasting physical activity are prone to injury. Therefore, prepare your athletes to withstand the exertion of playing your sport. An effective conditioning program for soccer would involve running and other forms of aerobic activity.

Make conditioning drills and activities fun. Include a skill component, such as dribbling, to prevent players from becoming bored or looking upon the activity as work.

Keep in mind, too, that players on your team may respond differently to conditioning activities. Wide-ranging levels of fitness or natural ability might mean that an activity that challenges one child is beyond another's ability to complete safely. The environment is another factor that may affect players' responses to activity. The same workout that was effective on a cool morning might be hazardous to players on a hot, humid afternoon. Similarly, an activity children excel in at sea level might present a risk at higher altitudes. An ideal conditioning program prepares players for the season's demands without neglecting physical and environmental factors that affect their safety.

Equipment and Facilities Inspection

Another way to prevent injuries is to check the quality and fit of all of the protective equipment used by your players. Inspect the equipment before you distribute it, after you have assigned the equipment, and regularly during the season. Ensure that all players have adequate shin pads and that they wear them. Worn-out, damaged, lost, or outdated equipment must be replaced immediately.

Remember, also, to examine regularly the field on which your players practice and play. Remove hazards, report conditions you cannot remedy, and request maintenance as necessary. If unsafe conditions exist, either make adaptations to avoid risk to your players' safety or stop the practice or match until safe conditions have been restored.

Matching Athletes by Maturity, and Warning of Inherent Risks

Children of the same age may differ in height and weight by up to 6 inches and 50 pounds. That's why in contact sports, or sports in which size provides an advantage, it's essential to match players against opponents of similar size and physical maturity. Such an approach gives smaller, less mature children a better chance to succeed and avoid injury, and provides larger children with more of a challenge.

Matching helps protect you from certain liability concerns. But you also must warn players of the inherent risks involved in playing soccer, because "failure to warn" is one of the most successful arguments in lawsuits against coaches. So, thoroughly explain the inherent risks of soccer, and make sure each player knows, understands, and appreciates those risks.

ASEP Fact

Soccer has one-half to one-fifth the injury rate of football and also has a lower injury rate than baseball and basketball for youths between the ages of 5 and 14.

The preseason parent orientation meeting is a good opportunity to explain the risks of the sport to parents and players. It is also a good occasion on which to have both the players and their parents sign waivers releasing you from liability should an injury occur. (See a sample Informed Consent Form on page 54.) Such waivers do not relieve you of responsibility for your players' well-being, but they are recommended by lawyers.

Proper Supervision and Record Keeping

With youngsters, your mere presence in the area of play is not enough; you must actively plan and direct team activities and closely observe and evaluate players' participation. You're the watchdog responsible for the players' well-being. So if you notice a player limping or grimacing, give him or her a rest and examine the extent of the injury.

INFORMED CONSENT FORM

I hereby give my permission for _____ to participate

in _____ during the athletic season beginning in 199____.
Further, I authorize the school to provide emergency treatment of an injury to or
illness of my child if qualified medical personnel consider treatment necessary *and*
perform the treatment. This authorization is granted only if I cannot be reached
and a reasonable effort has been made to do so.

Date _____ Parent or guardian _____

Address _____ Phone( )_____

Family physician _____ Phone ( )_____

Pre-existing medical conditions (e.g., allergies or chronic illnesses) _____

_____

Other(s) to also contact in case of emergency _____

Relationship to child _____ Phone ( )_____

My child and I are aware that participating in _____
is a potentially hazardous activity. I assume all risks associated with participation
in this sport, including but not limited to falls, contact with other participants, the
effects of the weather, traffic, and other reasonable risk conditions associated with
the sport. All such risks to my child are known and understood by me.

I understand this informed consent form and agree to its conditions on behalf of
my child.

Child's signature _____ Date _____

Parent's signature _____ Date _____

As a coach, you're also required to enforce the rules of the sport, prohibit dangerous horseplay, and hold practices only under safe weather conditions. These specific supervisory activities will make the play environment more safe for your players and will help protect you from liability if a mishap does occur.

For further protection, keep records of your season plans, practice plans, and players' injuries. Season and practice plans come in handy when you need evidence that players have been taught certain skills, whereas accurate, detailed accident report forms offer protection against unfounded lawsuits. Ask for these forms from the organization to which you belong. And hold onto these records for several years so that an "old soccer injury" of a former player doesn't come back to haunt you.

Providing Water Breaks

Encourage players to drink plenty of water before, during, and after practice. Because water makes up 45% to 65% of a youngster's body weight and water weighs about a pound per pint, the loss of even a little bit of water can have severe consequences for the body's systems. And it doesn't have to be hot and humid outside for players to become dehydrated. Nor do players have to feel thirsty; in fact, by the time they are aware of their thirst, they are long overdue for a drink.

Warm-Up and Cool-Down

Although young bodies are generally very limber, they, too, can get tight from inactivity. Therefore, a warm-up period of approximately 10 minutes before each practice is strongly recommended. Warm-up should address each muscle group and get the heart rate elevated in preparation for strenuous activity. Easy running followed by stretching activities is a common sequence.

As practice is winding down, slow players' heart rates with an easy jog or walk. Then arrange for a 5- to 10-minute period of easy stretching at the end of practice to help players avoid stiff muscles and make them less tight before the next practice.

What if One of My Players Gets Hurt?

No matter how good and thorough your prevention program, injuries will occur. When injury does strike, chances are you will be the one in charge. The severity and nature of the injury will determine how actively involved you'll be in treating the injury. But regardless of how seriously a player is hurt, it is your responsibility to know what steps to take. So let's look at how you can provide basic emergency care to your injured athletes.

ASEP Fact

Of all reported soccer injuries 75% are classified as minor injuries.

**Watch Out for Those
Legs and Feet!**

57% of all Soccer Injuries
Involve the Lower Extremities

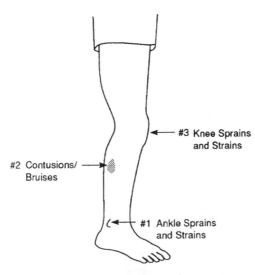

#3 Knee Sprains
and Strains

#2 Contusions/
Bruises

#1 Ankle Sprains
and Strains

The most common lower extremity injuries in soccer

Minor Injuries

Although no injury seems minor to the person experiencing it, most injuries are neither life-threatening nor severe enough to restrict participation. When such injuries occur, you can take an active role in their initial treatment.

Scrapes and Cuts

> ### ASEP Fact
>
> You shouldn't let a fear of acquired immune deficiency syndrome (AIDS) stop you from helping a player. On the field you are only at risk if you allow contaminated blood to come in contact with an open wound, so the blood barrier that you wear will protect you from AIDS should one of your players carry this disease. Check with your director or ASEP for more information about protecting yourself and your participants from AIDS.

When one of your players has an open wound, the first thing you should do is to put on a pair of disposable surgical gloves or some other effective blood barrier. Then follow these four steps:

1. Stop the bleeding by applying direct pressure with a clean dressing to the wound and elevating it. The player may be able to apply this pressure while you put on your gloves. Do not remove the dressing if it becomes soaked with blood. Instead, place an additional dressing on top of the one already in place. If bleeding continues, elevate the injured area above the heart and maintain pressure.

2. Cleanse the wound thoroughly once the bleeding is controlled. A good rinsing with a forceful stream of water, and perhaps light scrubbing with soap, will help prevent infection.

3. Protect the wound with sterile gauze or a bandage. If the player continues to participate, apply protective padding over the injured area.

4. <u>Remove and dispose of gloves</u> carefully to prevent you or anyone else from coming into contact with blood.

For bloody noses not associated with serious facial injury, have the athlete sit and lean slightly forward. Then pinch the player's nostrils shut. If the bleeding continues after several minutes, or if the athlete has a history of nosebleeds, seek medical assistance.

Strains and Sprains

The physical demands of soccer practices and games often result in injury to the muscles or tendons (strains), or to the ligaments (sprains). When your players suffer minor strains or sprains, immediately apply the PRICE method of injury care.

Bumps and Bruises

Inevitably, soccer players make contact with each other and with the ground. If the force of a body part at impact is great enough, a bump or bruise will result. Many players continue playing with such sore spots, but if the bump or bruise is large and painful, you should act appropriately. Enact the PRICE method of injury care and monitor the injury. If swelling, discoloration, and pain have lessened, the player may resume participation with protective padding; if not, the player should be examined by a physician.

Serious Injuries

Head, neck, and back injuries; fractures; and injuries that cause a player to lose consciousness are among a class of injuries that you cannot and should not try to treat yourself. But you should plan for what you'll do if such an injury occurs. And your plan should include the following guidelines for action:

- Obtain the phone number and ensure the availability of nearby emergency care units. Include this information as part of a written emergency plan before the season, and have it with you at every practice and match.

- Assign an assistant coach or another adult the responsibility of knowing the location of the nearest phone and contacting emergency medical help upon your request.

The PRICE Method

P— Protect the athlete and injured body part from further danger or further trauma.

R— Rest the area to avoid further damage and foster healing.

I— Ice the area to reduce swelling and pain.

C— Compress the area by securing an ice bag in place with an elastic wrap.

E— Elevate the injury above heart level to keep the blood from pooling in the area.

- Ensure that emergency medical information, treatment, and transportation consent forms are available during every practice and match.

- Do not move the injured athlete.

- Calm the injured athlete and keep others away from him or her as much as possible.

- Evaluate whether the athlete's breathing is stopped or irregular, and if necessary, clear the airway with your fingers.

- Administer artificial respiration if breathing is stopped. Administer cardiopulmonary resuscitation (CPR), or have a trained individual administer CPR, if the athlete's circulation has stopped.

- Remain with the athlete until medical personnel arrive.

How Do I Protect Myself?

When one of your players is injured, naturally your first concern is his or her well-being. Your feelings for children, after all, are what made you decide to coach. Unfortunately, there is something else that you must consider: Can you be held liable for the injury?

From a legal standpoint, a coach has nine duties to fulfill. We've discussed all but planning (see unit 4) in this unit:

1. Provide a safe environment.

2. Properly plan the activity.

3. Provide adequate and proper equipment.

4. Match or equate athletes.

5. Warn of inherent risks in the sport.

6. Supervise the activity closely.

7. Evaluate athletes for injury or incapacitation.

8. Know emergency procedures and first aid.

9. Keep adequate records.

In addition to fulfilling these nine legal duties, you should check your insurance coverage to make sure your policy will protect you from liability.

Summary Self-Test

Now that you've read how to make your coaching experience safe for your players and yourself, test your knowledge of the material by answering these questions:

1. What are eight injury-prevention measures you can institute to try to keep your players from getting hurt?
2. What is the four-step emergency care process for cuts?
3. What method of treatment is best for minor sprains and strains?
4. What steps can you take to manage serious injuries?
5. What are the nine legal duties of a coach?

Unit 6

What Is Soccer All About?

From reading the first part of this manual, you now have a good, general understanding of what it takes to coach. Now it's time to develop your comprehension of soccer. This part of the book provides the soccer-specific information you will need to teach your players the sport.

Advantages of Soccer

You may be less familiar with soccer than with some other sports, but soccer has many advantages over other activities. Here are some of the reasons we ADVISE youth sport programs to include soccer:

A—Able to be played year-round, indoors and out

D—Develops individual skills and teamwork

V—Vigorous and continuous exercise

I—Inexpensive, with few equipment or facility requirements

S—Safe, noncollision sport

E—Easy to learn and play

However, the most positive thing about soccer is that kids love it. So even though your previous soccer experience may be limited, be enthusiastic about teaching this sport. And prepare for it by reading the rest of this manual and consulting other sources for more soccer information.

ASEP Fact

Soccer is played by more than 7 million 6- to 11-year-olds, making it the second most popular team sport among kids in this country.

Approaches to Soccer

Most coaches are acquainted with regulation soccer, consisting of 11 players on each team. However, beginning coaches should also be aware of two other approaches to this game — small-sided soccer and indoor soccer. Small-sided games with seven or eight players on a side may, in fact, be the perfect starting place for the beginning player.

Regulation Soccer

Regulation soccer is played with 11 on a side. Each team consists of one goalkeeper and 10 field players whose objective is two-fold: to score a goal against the opponent and to prevent the opposition from scoring on them. Positions, as explained on pages 70–71, include those of defenders, midfielders, forwards, and goalkeepers.

Small-Sided Soccer

Small-sided games can be used to develop individual player skills. However, small-sided games can also be played as an alternative to regulation or indoor soccer. In fact, they provide an ideal starting place for the very young player. In small-sided soccer, each team generally consists of anywhere from three to six players. The team objectives for this kind of soccer are the same as those for regulation soccer: to score on the other team while preventing the opposition from making a goal. Field dimensions vary. Three versus three is generally played without goalkeepers on a field that is considerably smaller than the one used in regulation soccer. Six versus six, seven versus seven, or eight versus eight, on the other hand, is generally played with a goalkeeper. The remaining players occupy positions on the field.

Indoor Soccer

Indoor soccer is similar to a six-versus-six small-sided game. Each team consists of a goalie and five field players, who may be set up in one of the formations discussed later in this unit on pages 71–74 (see Figure 6.5a–c). The main difference between indoor soccer and small-sided games is that indoor soccer represents a blend of hockey and soccer. Thus, because the field of play is generally surrounded by a wall, play is continuous, and the ball may be played off the boards surrounding the playing area.

In indoor soccer, substitutions occur while play is in progress. Play is not temporarily halted while coaches make their substitutions, and there are no throw-ins or corner kicks. If the ball goes out-of-bounds, the team that didn't touch the ball last takes a free kick at that point, inbounds, where the ball left the playing field. There is also no offside rule in indoor soccer, and players who commit fouls may have to sit out for two to five minutes, during which time their team has to play one short until the penalty period expires or the other team scores a goal. Indoor soccer can be a very fast-paced game. Like small-sided soccer, it requires greater skill and helps players develop the skill to play on a more competitive level.

Differences and Similarities in Soccer Formations

On the surface, regulation soccer is similar to small-sided and indoor soccer. The objectives remain the same. Even so, small-sided and indoor soccer can perhaps be best understood if considered in relation to regulation soccer.

For one thing, regulation soccer should be a passing game—players need to advance the ball down the field using a combination of long and short passes. Small-sided soccer and indoor soccer, on the other hand, call for shorter, more controlled passes because of the limited spaces in which they are played.

Furthermore, because it is played on a much larger field, regulation soccer is not as fast paced as the other types and does not require as much precision in passing, trapping, and so on. Thus, a mistake on defense—a missed tackle, for instance—may not be costly in regulation soccer; players have room for mistakes. But in small-sided and indoor games, with fewer players, mistakes in front of the goal often result in a scoring opportunity for the other team.

In regulation soccer, players can actually use the size of the field to their advantage. For instance, if the defenders can keep the ball out of the middle and to the outside, it is difficult for the attacking team to score. However, in indoor and small-sided soccer, the diminished field size makes it possible for the attacking team to score from anywhere near the goal.

Finally, regulation soccer requires more stamina than small-sided or indoor soccer. However, regulation soccer does not require the speed or quickness of small-sided and indoor soccer.

Advantages and Disadvantages in Soccer Formations

The advantage of small-sided and indoor soccer is that they allow coach and players year-round play. While this year-round play may result in burnout in some cases, it helps the development of skill and increases understanding of the game, thus making it easier for the committed player to move to a more competitive level. One disadvantage of taking a regulation team into an indoor or small-sided league is that players may develop habits that could spell disaster in regulation soccer. For instance, while small-sided and indoor soccer emphasize short, controlled passing, the same sort of passing in front of one's own goal in regulation soccer could easily provide a scoring opportunity for the opposition. Also, indoor and small-sided soccer encourage dribbling, but the same amount of individual dribbling in a regulation outdoor match may considerably weaken a team's attack and endanger the defense.

Age and Skill Guidelines

Which approach to soccer is best for your team? The age of your youngsters and the number of years they have played soccer can help you determine the answer. Table 6.1 matches the three approaches to soccer with age and years of experience. For example, small-sided soccer games requiring seven or eight on a side provide an ideal starting point for the young, inexperienced player. Fewer players and a more restricted field size allow each player more "touches" on the ball.

Table 6.1 Soccer Age and Skill Guidelines		
Age	Years played	Recommended approach
6–9	0–2	Small-sided soccer
10–12	0–2	Small-sided and regulation soccer
10–12	2–4	Small-sided, regulation, and indoor soccer
13–15	0–2	Small-sided and regulation soccer
13–15	2–4	Small-sided, indoor, and regulation soccer
10–15	5–6	Small-sided, indoor, and regulation soccer

Of course, it is difficult to say precisely at what age a youth should begin regulation or indoor soccer. The coach is the best judge.

What Are the Rules?

Soccer is generally played using the rules established by the Fédération Internationale de Football Associations (FIFA). Your organization might have some modifications to the FIFA's rules, so be sure to do your homework.

Ball and Field Dimensions

Soccer is a game in which a ball is passed, dribbled, and shot using any part of the body except the hands. The regulation soccer ball is a size 5, but many youth soccer leagues use a size 4 ball, which is easier for smaller participants to play with. Similarly, scaled-down fields and goals are preferred for younger, smaller players.

Small-sided games and indoor soccer are played in areas quite a bit smaller than that used for regulation soccer. For instance, three versus three may be played in an area approximately 30 by 20 yards or even smaller. Six versus six, on the other hand, may be played in an area that is a little smaller than half the size of a regulation playing field. The dimensions of an indoor soccer field are the same as those for ice hockey (see Figure 6.1). Table 6.2 offers recommendations regarding field and goal dimensions for youth soccer.

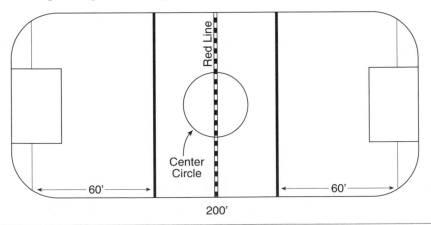

■ **Figure 6.1**   The dimensions of an indoor soccer field are the same as those for ice hockey.

Table 6.2 Fitting the Field to the Players		
Players' ages	**Field size**	**Goal size**
13 and older	100–120 yd long 55–75 wide	8 ft high 8 yd wide
9–12	80 yd long 55 yd wide	7 ft high 7 yd wide
6–8	70 yd long 50 yd wide	6 ft high 6 yd wide

Field Markings

Regardless of the size of the field, specific areas are designated for certain game activities. Take time to familiarize yourself with the field markings illustrated in Figure 6.2.

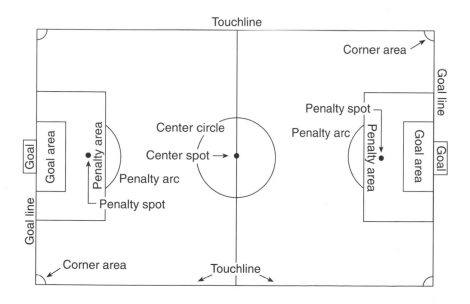

■ **Figure 6.2**   Soccer field of play.

Player Equipment

Soccer requires very little equipment. Multi-studded soccer shoes are recommended for outdoors, whereas tennis shoes work well indoors. Clothing should be loose fitting and appropriate for weather conditions. Socks are needed to hold in place the shin guards players must wear to protect their legs. Goalies' jerseys should be of a different color than teammates'. And because of the demands of the position, goalkeepers should wear extra padding at the elbows and hips.

Player Positions

Soccer is played with 11 players per team; however, many youth leagues consist of 7-, 8-, or 9-player teams. Each player, at times, plays offense (trying to score) and defense (trying to steal the ball and prevent the other team from scoring). The four main positions in soccer are forward, midfielder, defender, and goalkeeper (see Figure 6.3).

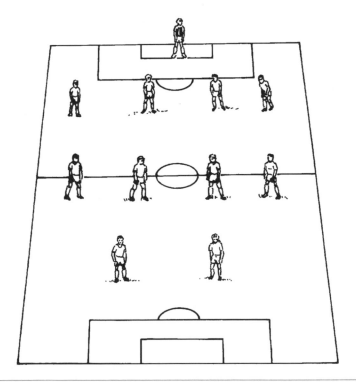

■ **Figure 6.3** Player positions.

Forwards

Forwards play closer to the other team's goal and shoot the ball more than do other players. The forwards that play nearest the touchlines are called "wings"; those in the middle of the field are referred to as "strikers." Teams usually play with one or two forwards in their lineups.

Midfielders

Midfielders, or halfbacks, are all-purpose players, who take shots and also try to steal the ball from the other team. Their position is named appropriately, as they are located between forwards and defenders on the field. Teams use three to five midfielders throughout the game.

Defenders

Defenders, or fullbacks, play near their own team's goal and try to prevent the other team from shooting the ball. They also receive the ball from the goalie and move the ball up the field to begin the offense. Teams typically use three to five defenders during the game.

Goalkeeper

A goalie plays in front of the goal and tries to prevent the ball from getting into the goal. The goalie is the only player allowed to use the hands for such things as blocking shots and initiating the offense from within the goal area.

Team Formations

Currently, the most popular full-field team "formation" is the 4-4-2: four defenders, four midfielders, and two forwards. This formation works for more experienced teams whose midfielders know that, on attack, they must make "runs" to the forward position to create scoring opportunities. However, beginning players may have trouble with the 4-4-2 and may feel more comfortable playing in one of the following team formations:

- 4-3-3: four defenders, three midfielders, and three forwards (see Figure 6.4a),
- 4-2-4: four defenders, two midfielders, and four forwards (see Figure 6.4b), or
- 3-3-4: three defenders, three midfielders, and four forwards (see Figure 6.4c)

A team using the 4-2-4 can always drop one of its forwards back to midfield while a team using the 3-3-4 can bring one of its midfielders back to help on defense.

a

b

c

■ **Figure 6.4** Beginning players may have more success playing in either the (a) 4-3-3, (b) 4-2-4, or (c) 3-3-4 team formation.

Player positions for small-sided games and indoor soccer are similar. If you have entered a team into a six versus six league, you may wish to try a 1-2-2 formation that consists of three defenders and two attackers or a 2-1-2, which consists of two defenders, one midfielder, and two attackers (see Figures 6.5a and b). Another possibility is the 2-2-1 formation, which consists of two defenders, two midfielders, and one attacker (see Figure 6.5c). Keep in mind that no one set formation exists. As in regulation soccer, use the formation that is best suited to the strengths and weaknesses of the team.

Officials

A soccer game should be officiated by two or three individuals who have knowledge of all of the rules and enforce those rules to ensure a safe, fair, and fun contest. Officials should also require sportsmanship from each player *and* the coaches. You can be a big help to officials by acting with character and emphasizing to your players the need to play with discipline. The illustrations in Appendix B show the signals used by soccer officials during a game. Familiarize yourself with these signals and teach them to your players.

a

b

c

■ **Figure 6.5** Possible small-sided and indoor soccer team formations: (a) 1-2-2, (b) 2-1-2, and (c) 2-2-1.

Length of the Game

A soccer game consists of two halves or four quarters and intermissions of varying length, depending on the guidelines of your local organization. The length of the game should be adjusted according to the ages of the players. Youngsters 12 or under should play halves of no longer than 30 minutes' duration. The clock is stopped only when a player is injured.

Starting and Restarting the Game

In regulation soccer, a coin toss determines which team has the choice of kicking off or deciding what goal to defend. Soccer games begin with one team kicking the ball from the center spot. The opposing team's players are not allowed within the center circle during the kickoff. Players on both teams must be on their half of the field during the kickoff, and the kicked ball must roll forward at least one complete rotation before another player can touch it.

These same kickoff procedures are followed after a goal is scored. In this situation, the team that was scored against restarts the game by kicking off from the center spot, and the team that scored stands outside of the center circle in its half of the field.

Play also stops when the ball is kicked out-of-bounds or when an official calls a foul. The procedure used to restart the game after an out-of-bounds will be one of the following, depending on where the ball left the field of play:

- *Goal kick*
- *Corner kick*
- *Throw-in*

Goal Kick

When an attacking team kicks the ball out-of-bounds beyond the goal line, which often happens on a missed shot, the opposing team is awarded a free kick, called a *goal kick*. This kick is made by the defending team and must be made inside the goal box on the side of the goal on which the ball went out of play. The players on the team that kicked the ball out-of-bounds must stay outside the penalty area (see Figure 6.6).

■ **Figure 6.6** Goal kick.

Corner Kick

If a team kicks the ball beyond its own goal line, the other team is awarded a corner kick from a corner arc. During the kick, defensive players must be at least 10 yards from the player kicking the ball. The kicker's teammates can position themselves anywhere they choose (see Figure 6.7).

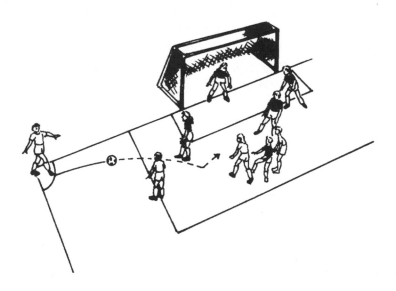

■ **Figure 6.7** Corner kick.

Throw-In

When the ball is kicked out-of-bounds along the touchline, the game is restarted with a throw-in (see Figure 6.8). The team that last touched the ball loses possession, and the other team gets to throw in the ball. The player putting the ball back in play must use both hands to throw the ball and keep both feet on the ground. The player should arch the back as far back as possible to help snap the ball forward. The throwing motion should begin from behind the head and be a continuous forward thrust until the ball is released in front of the head. The throw-in should be put into play quickly, thrown to an unmarked player, and passed in a manner that is easy to control.

■ **Figure 6.8**   Throw-in.

In small-sided soccer, restarts are similar to those allowed in regulation soccer. Players do throw-ins, take goal kicks, and kick off just as they do in regulation soccer. Because of the very restricted space in which indoor soccer is played, however, throw-ins and corner kicks are not part of the game. In all kinds of soccer, direct and indirect free kicks resulting from player fouls are allowed, and a handball or a trip in the penalty area should be penalized by awarding a penalty kick.

Fouls

Fouls are called when one player runs into, charges, pushes, trips, kicks, or holds an opposing player. A handball foul is called when a player intentionally touches the ball with his or her hand or arm to gain control.

An offside foul is called when a teammate tries to pass the ball to a player in the offside position. A player is in the offside position when the player gets closer to the opponents' goal than at least two defensive players (including the goalie). The offside rule prevents offensive players from simply waiting at the goal mouth for an easy shot, but it does not apply to throw-in or corner kick situations.

In soccer, players who intentionally foul or play dangerously are warned once by an official, who presents them with a yellow card. The next time they intentionally foul or play dangerously, they receive a red card and are ejected from the game. Officials can also eject a player without warning if they rule a behavior unacceptable.

Free Kicks

Fouls result in either a direct or an indirect free kick (see Table 6.3). Direct free kicks can be kicked directly at the goal, whereas indirect free kicks must touch another player before a goal can be scored. The officials will signal which free kick has been awarded.

Table 6.3 Free Kick Fouls	
This chart will help you remember which fouls receive a direct or an indirect free kick.	
Direct kick	**Indirect kick**
Handball	Playing dangerously
Kicking an opponent	Obstructing an opponent
Striking an opponent	Goalkeeper taking too many steps
Tripping an opponent	(four or more)
Holding an opponent	Offside
Pushing an opponent	
Jumping at an opponent	
Charging into an opponent	
Charging from behind	

Penalty Kicks

Penalty kicks are awarded to the attacking team if a defending player commits a direct-kick foul inside the penalty area. A penalty kick is a free shot at the goal by an individual attacker with only the goalkeeper defending against the shot. Penalty kicks are taken 12 yards in front of the center of the goal (see Figure 6.9). The goalkeeper cannot leave the line until after the ball is kicked.

■ **Figure 6.9**   Penalty kick.

Scoring

Each time the entire ball crosses the goal line between the goalposts, the offensive team is awarded one goal. Scoring a goal is a thrill for a youngster, and it is one of the tangible ways to measure personal performance. However, don't overemphasize goal scoring in assessing a player's contribution. Give equal attention to players who make assists, tackles, or saves, or who demonstrate leadership, sportsmanship, and effort.

Summary Test

Now that you've read the basic soccer information in this unit, you should be able to answer a number of questions about the sport. To test yourself, match up each of the following quiz questions with the correct response:

a. Penalty kick   f. Goalkeeper
b. Corner kick   g. Throw-in
c. Forwards   h. Goal kick
d. Direct free kick   i. Indirect free kick
e. Midfielders   j. Defenders

1. _____ Is awarded after a foul, such as a handball, and does not have to touch a teammate before a goal can be scored.

2. _____ Teams usually use three to five players of this position to try to prevent the opposing team from scoring.

3. _____ A free shot awarded to an attacking team if a defender commits a direct-kick foul within the penalty area.

4. _____ Players on the team who shoot the ball the most.

5. _____ Awarded to an attacking team when the defending team causes the ball to go beyond its *own* goal line.

6. _____ The only position in which players are allowed to use their hands.

7. _____ Awarded to a team when the opposing team was last to touch the ball before it went out-of-bounds on the touchline.

8. _____ All-purpose players whose responsibilities include taking shots and attempting to gain possession of the ball from the opposition.

9. _____ Awarded to the defending team when an attacking team causes the ball to go beyond the goal line.

10. _____ Is awarded after a foul, such as an offside foul, and requires that the ball be touched by another player before a goal can be scored.

Answers: 1. d, 2. j, 3. a, 4. c, 5. b, 6. f, 7. g, 8. e, 9. h, 10. i.

What Soccer Skills and Drills Should I Teach?

In unit 4 you learned *how* to teach soccer skills using the IDEA method (see pages 36–40) and plan for practices. Now it's time to consider exactly *what* soccer skills to emphasize and what activities to use to help your players develop these skills. This unit describes the basic skills, suggests how to organize players on the practice field during drills, and recommends a variety of drills and small-sided games that you can use to develop your players' soccer skills.

What Soccer Skills Are Important?

This section describes the basic soccer skills you'll want your players to learn. Emphasize each skill equally so that your young athletes become well-rounded soccer players.

Ready Position

The most basic soccer skill is the ready position. Instruct your players to stand relaxed with their arms and legs shoulders' width apart and slightly bent, balanced on the balls of their feet, with one leg slightly in front of the other (see Figure 7.1). From this position a player can easily run forward, backward, or to either side. A player can also more easily kick, trap (receive and control), and head the ball from the ready position. So, from the very first practice, have your players assume and maintain an alert stance on the field.

Offensive Skills

A key to soccer success is controlling the ball so that your team, and not the opposition, can score. Therefore the ability to pass, trap, and shoot the ball is essential.

Figure 7.1   Ready position.

Passing

Passing the ball among teammates is an offensive skill used to maintain possession and create scoring opportunities. Passes should be short and crisp; long or slow passes are likely to be stolen by an opposing player. However, players should avoid using passes that are too hard and difficult to control.

Short passes are kicked with the inside of the foot. The correct technique for such passes has several stages:

1. Plant the nonkicking foot alongside and near the ball (see Figure 7.2a).

2. Square up the hips and shoulders to the teammate for whom the pass is intended.

3. Turn out the kicking foot (see Figure 7.2b).

4. Swing the kicking foot straight at the center of the ball (see Figure 7.2c).

5. Follow through by swinging the kicking leg well beyond the point of impact with the ball, in the direction of the teammate to whom the ball is being passed (see Figure 7.2d).

a

b

c

d

■ **Figure 7.2** Sequence for short passes: (a) Plant the nonkicking foot, (b) turn out the kicking foot, (c) swing the foot at the center of the ball, and (d) follow through.

Sometimes a game situation will call for a player to make a long pass to a teammate across the field. The best way for your players to make long passes is to *loft* the ball through the air using the top of the foot. You can teach this technique by emphasizing four keys to lofting passes:

- Plant the nonkicking foot slightly behind and to the side of the ball (see Figure 7.3a).

- Point the toes of the kicking foot down, and kick the ball with the shoelace area.

- Kick under the ball (see Figure 7.3b).

- Watch the kicking foot contact the bottom half of the ball and lift it off the ground (see Figure 7.3c).

■ **Figure 7.3** Sequence for long passes: (a) Plant the nonkicking foot slightly behind and to the side of the ball, (b) kick under the ball, and (c) watch the kicking foot contact the bottom half of the ball and lift it off the ground.

Players should learn to use the outside of the foot to pass to the side. However, this technique may be uncomfortable and difficult for young players to perform. Young players also find the instep, or power, pass difficult; they tend to use their toes, an incorrect technique. You may want to have players learn these types of passes after they're proficient at the short and long passes.

Error Detection and Correction for Passing

A common problem for young soccer players is getting passes to go where they are intended to go. If you spot a player always passing erratically, take the time to repeat instruction in the proper technique.

ERROR: Lack of accuracy

CORRECTION

1. Plant nonkicking foot beside the ball with toes pointed toward teammate who is to receive pass.
2. Square shoulders and hips to the receiver (see Figure 7.4).
3. Keep the kicking foot firm throughout the kicking motion.
4. Follow through with the kicking foot.

■ **Figure 7.4**   Squaring up to the target.

Trapping

Receiving and controlling passes is called *trapping*. A player can trap the ball with just about any part of the body. Here are some key components to trapping:

- Get in front of the ball.
- Watch the ball.
- Cushion the ball.
- Keep the ball near the body.

The following are more specific pointers you can give your players on trapping with the foot, thigh, and chest:

Foot Trap. To trap the ball on or near the ground with the foot, a player should stand in front of the ball and extend a leg and foot out to meet it. After the ball reaches the player's foot, he or she should pull the leg back to slow the ball and relax the foot when the ball makes contact. This technique is called *cushioning* the ball. If a player does not cushion the ball, it will bounce away from the foot, and the player will lose control. The inside-of-foot trap (see Figure 7.5) provides the most surface area and is best for beginning players. Eventually, players should learn how to trap with the outside and top of both feet. Note that players performing this latter form of foot trap should also use the lower shin and front part of the ankle to cushion the ball.

■ **Figure 7.5** Inside-of-foot trap.

Error Detection and Correction for Foot Traps

Players learning how to trap are often frustrated by their inability to control the ball after making contact with it. Perhaps the easiest trap to learn how to control is the inside-of-foot trap. Teach players this technique to increase their confidence in other types of traps.

ERROR: Losing control of the ball off the foot

CORRECTION

1. Contact the bottom and side of the ball with the inside of the foot—midway between the heel and toes.
2. Cushion the impact of the ball by withdrawing the foot immediately before contact (see Figure 7.6).

■ **Figure 7.6**   Inside-of-foot trap.

Thigh Trap.   The thigh can be used to trap a ball in the air when players stand in front of the ball and flex one knee. The thigh of the raised leg should be used to stop the flight of the ball and keep it in the receiving player's vicinity (see Figure 7.7a). Players can cushion the ball by dropping the knee slightly as the ball touches the thigh (see Figure 7.7b). This technique will keep the ball from bouncing away (see Figure 7.7c).

■ **Figure 7.7**   Thigh trap: (a) Stop the ball with the thigh of the raised leg, (b) cushion the ball by dropping the knee slightly, and (c) keep the ball from bouncing away.

Chest Trap.   A player can also use the chest to trap the ball. The player should stand in the ball's line of flight, with arms held up for balance and chest pushed out to meet the ball (see Figures 7.8a and b). When the ball contacts the body, the player should pull the chest back to cushion the ball (see Figure 7.8c).

■ **Figure 7.8**   Chest trap: (a and b) Stand in the ball's line of flight, with the arms held up and chest pushed out to meet the ball, and (c) pull the chest back to cushion the ball when it contacts the body.

Dribbling

Players must learn how to control the ball with their feet. Dribbling can be used to move the ball down the field for a pass or shot, to keep the ball from the opposing team, or to change direction.

Players need to be able to use both the insides and outsides of their feet to dribble. To dribble with the inside of the foot, players must turn the foot out and push the ball forward as they move (see Figure 7.9a). To dribble with the outside of the foot, players must turn the foot in and push the ball slightly forward or to the side (see Figure 7.9b).

a   b

■ **Figure 7.9**   (a) Inside- and (b) outside-of-foot dribbles.

Dribbling may be difficult at first. Have players start by walking and dribbling. Once they can perform the skill correctly, they can speed up their dribbling pace. Insist that players try to look up as they dribble and not down at the ball. If they always look down, they are likely to have the ball stolen by an opponent and are not likely to see a teammate who is open to receive a pass. Encourage players to use either foot to dribble—they'll be more likely to protect the ball from opponents.

As they improve, have your players dribble against an opponent. Being marked by a defender will require them to vary speed, change direction, and shield the ball. Have them prepare for defensive pressure by practicing speeding up and slowing down as they dribble and by dribbling around towels or cones, as shown in Figure 7.10.

■ **Figure 7.10** Dribbling practice.

Here are the keys to dribbling you'll want to emphasize:

- Push the ball softly in the desired direction if dribbling in close proximity to defenders.
- Look up and watch for other players.
- Keep the ball close to the feet. If it is too far ahead, other players can steal it.
- Shield the ball from opponents.
- Run at a speed at which the ball can be controlled.
- If speed dribbling, push the ball out several feet ahead and sprint to the ball.

Young soccer players have difficulty dribbling the ball consistently and under control. Work with them to develop a feel for the ball so they are able to maintain possession of it.

ERROR: Letting the ball get too far away to keep possession

CORRECTION

1. Keep the ball underneath the body, close to the feet.

2. Nudge the ball gently in different directions, never letting it get more than a stride's length away.

3. Determine whether the grass or ball require adjustments. A very inflated ball or very short grass will cause the ball to roll faster and farther.

Heading

Heading is the alternative to kicking the ball for passes or shots and can be used by defenders to clear the ball from an area of attack. It's a technique your players will have to use their heads for, literally. Heading is a skill that is less used because it is so often incorrectly taught, and what the players don't know, they can't use.

Therefore, what you teach players about heading should be technically correct. Give players the following tips for heading the ball:

*   Be balanced and relaxed with the feet slightly apart (see Figure 7.11a). Pull the head and body back and move to the ball.

*   Keep the eyes open and mouth closed. Gaping jaws can cause players to bite their tongues.

*   Thrust the body forward to meet the ball, hitting it with the forehead at the hairline (see Figure 7.11b). Meet the ball, don't wait for it.

*   Clench the neck muscles, keeping the neck firm while driving forward (see Figure 7.11c).

■ **Figure 7.11**   Heading: (a) Be balanced and relaxed, (b) hit the ball with the forehead at the hairline, and (c) keep the neck firm while driving forward.

Shooting

Every player likes to score goals, so your players will be highly motivated to learn proper shooting technique. Point out to them the similarities of shooting and passing; shots also come from the inside, top, and outside of the foot and from heading the ball. Also mention some of these key differences between passing and shooting:

- *Length*—Shots often must travel a greater distance than passes because defenders work at keeping offensive players away from the goal.

- *Speed*—Shooters frequently kick the ball harder than passers do, so the goalie cannot react to stop the shot. Unlike the passer, the shooter doesn't need to be concerned whether a teammate can control the kick.

- *Purpose*—Shots are taken for one reason: to score a goal. On the other hand, players pass the ball for many different reasons (e.g., to get a better shot and to keep the ball away from the defense).

Instruct your players to shoot away from the goalie and toward the corners of the goal. Finally, tell your players to shoot often. Nothing puts greater pressure on a defensive team than shots on goal.

Error Detection and Correction for Shooting

Youngsters often shoot too soft or miss the goal because of improper mechanics. When you see poor shooting technique, be prepared to intervene with helpful suggestions.

ERROR: Slow and inaccurate shots

CORRECTION

1. Square shoulders and hips to the goal.
2. Keep kicking leg cocked until the nonkicking foot is firmly planted beside the ball.
3. Strike the ball forcefully with the foot.
4. Watch the ball as it leaves the kicking foot.
5. Follow through completely, keeping the kicking leg pointing goalward well beyond the point of impact (see Figure 7.12).

■ **Figure 7.12**   Follow through on the shot.

Defensive Skills

The individual defensive skills of soccer are perhaps less glamorous than individual offensive techniques such as shooting. However, it is equally important to teach players the defensive techniques needed to develop all-around soccer skills. So let's examine the defensive skills you'll want your players to learn and perform.

Stance and Footwork

The ready position described on page 82 is the best defensive stance. This stance allows the defender to move quickly in any direction and to maintain balance.

Defensive players often need to move in short, quick, lateral bursts. Therefore, have your players practice sliding or side-stepping quickly from one point to another, *without* crossing one leg over the other (see Figure 7.13).

■ **Figure 7.13**   Defensive slide.

At other times, defensive players must turn and run to catch an elusive opponent or to gain possession of the ball. In such instances, players should use the crossover step. Teach them to plant and push off the foot nearest to the opponent or ball (see Figure 7.14a), then swing the opposite leg in front of the body as they turn in the intended direction (see Figures 7.14b and c).

a   b   c

■ **Figure 7.14** Crossover step: (a) Plant and push off the foot nearest to the opponent or ball, (b) swing the opposite leg in front of the body, and (c) turn in the intended direction.

Marking

Offensive players must be guarded to prevent them from scoring. Defenders should try to mark or guard the player to whom they are assigned, staying near that offensive player and between the ball and the goal. From this position, defensive players will be able to gain possession of the ball off the dribble and intercept passes. Marking is generally used to slow down an opponent and allow teammates to recover to their positions.

Get your players to notice opponents' habits (see Figure 7.15), such as using only one leg to dribble, pass, or shoot. Then they'll be able to overplay the offensive players to whom they are assigned and perhaps block or gain possession of the ball frequently.

■ **Figure 7.15**　Recognizing a dribbler's habits.

Tackling

Taking the ball from an offensive player is called *tackling*. Players should not be afraid to attempt to take the ball when they have a good opportunity—for example, when the dribbler pushes the ball too far ahead. Defenders should, however, be prepared to reestablish position if they are unsuccessful in their take-away attempts. Also, fullbacks should be certain that they have teammates backing them up before attempting to tackle near midfield.

Teach players to *time* their tackles; ideally, they should step in when the attacker temporarily loses control of the ball. Lunging at the ball—or "diving in"—is a dangerous tactic to teach, even at a very young age. A good dribbler will usually go around a defender who lunges at the ball with no trouble. When positioning to make a tackle, the defender should approach the dribbler in a sideways position. If this technique is followed, the attacker cannot push the ball between the defender's legs. And remember, tell your players to go for the ball—not the opponent.

Error Detection and Correction for Marking

Defensive skills are frequently neglected by youth soccer players. Encourage your players to use proper technique when attempting to gain possession of the ball and to take pride in keeping opponents from scoring.

ERROR: Letting the offensive player get by with the dribble, as in Figure 7.16

CORRECTION

1. Maintain ready position.
2. Calculate and respect the dribbler's speed and ability and adjust marking distance accordingly.
3. Don't get fooled by head fakes—watch the ball.
4. Attempt tackles of the ball only when the ball is off the dribbler's foot.

■ **Figure 7.16**   Error in marking a dribbler.

Goalkeeping

Playing goalie is fun and challenging. The goalkeeper must be alert and watch the ball at all times. As the last line of defense to prevent a goal, the goalkeeper perhaps has the greatest individual defensive responsibility on the team. Remember that this responsibility also increases goalkeepers' chances for injury. Contact your league administrator to see what special equipment and safety instructions your goalies need to play safely.

Error Detection and Correction for Tackling

The word *tackle* will cause some players to cringe and others to cheer. However, tackling in soccer is not the same as in football. Point out the difference as you describe how improper tackling is both dangerous and damaging to the defense.

ERROR: Overextending a leg in attempting a tackle

CORRECTION

1. Mark the dribbler as closely as possible and look for an opportunity to take possession of the ball (see Figure 7.17a).
2. If the dribbler is careless or unskilled, take advantage by tackling the ball.
3. Gain position by planting the nonkicking leg near the ball (see Figure 7.17b). Then use a short, firm kick with the other leg to knock it away from the opponent (see Figure 7.17c).

a   b   c

■ **Figure 7.17**   Proper tackling sequence.

The best way for goalies to stop a shot is to catch the ball. Goalies should use the basic "W" catch to catch balls shot shoulder height and higher (see Figure 7.18). This position requires the fingers to be spread and the hands to come together in front of the head. If goalies cannot catch the ball, they should kick it or punch it away with a fist or leg. When catching the ball, the goalkeeper should pull it tightly to the body. Remember, goalies can use their hands only inside the penalty area (see field diagram on page 69). Within this zone, they are allowed four steps to throw or kick the ball to a teammate.

The outlet pass or kick should be accurate and of a speed that allows a teammate to handle it easily. However, the goalie must put enough speed on the ball and vary the delivery so opponents aren't able to anticipate and intercept the outlet.

■ **Figure 7.18** Goalkeeper defending an above-the-shoulder shot.

Have goalies assume a position 1 or 2 yards in front of the goal. Remind them to watch the ball carefully and to maintain the ready position. Factors like field size and speed require indoor soccer goalies to play close to the net; outdoor goalies can be more involved in field play. Teach your goalkeepers to move about in front of the goal on an imaginary semicircle. When the ball is in the center part of the field, the goalies should be slightly farther from the goal than when it is at an angle. In either case, the goalie should be positioned to decrease the shooting angle between the ball and the goal and remain between the two goal posts.

Goalies especially need to work on their lateral movement and quickness. They'll need this agility to recover quickly to defend against rebound shots and chip passes near the goal. You can use the goalkeeping drills on pages 117–119 to help your goalies develop their footwork and reaction to the ball.

Now that you know the basic individual soccer skills, you probably want to know what drills to use to develop these skills in your players. Before jumping right into the drills, however, consider how you are going to set up your practice sessions to make such activities productive and efficient.

Error Detection and Correction for Goalkeeping

Goalkeeping is a difficult task, especially for small players who have trouble handling the ball. Although physical growth will remedy some of a young goalkeeper's problems, proper technique instruction can solve even more.

ERROR: Low, hard shots bouncing off the hands in front of the goal

CORRECTION

1. Square up to the shooter and be in the ready position.
2. Don't try to control low, hard shots only with the hands (see Figures 7.19a and b).
3. Let the ball roll up onto the wrists and forearms (see Figure 7.19c).
4. Clutch the ball to the chest (see Figure 7.19d).

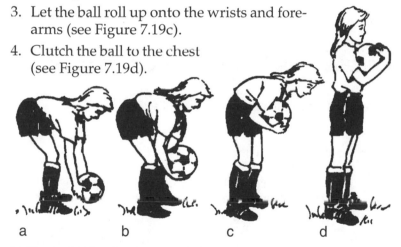

a   b   c   d

■ **Figure 7.19**   Goalkeeper defending low, hard shot.

How Do I Use Soccer Drills Effectively?

Dividing the practice field into a series of grids is a good method for organizing practice sessions and conducting drills (see Figure 7.20). This grid system can be arranged using cones or other markers to mark plots on the field. Have players pair up and practice skills inside individual grids. Two or more grids can also be combined to play small-sided games or to practice skills that require more room.

Ensure that each grid area has a sufficient number of balls for all players to keep active. Once your players are organized on the field, they can simultaneously perform drills that will improve their skills.

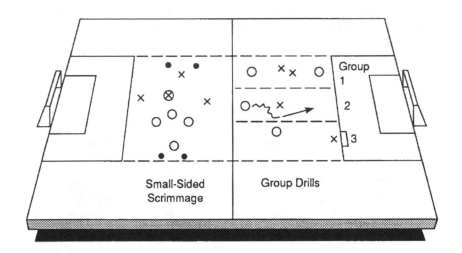

Figure 7.20 Grid system for practice drills.

Here are some tips for using soccer drills:

⟹ *Use individual and partner drills frequently.* These types of drills give each player the opportunity to handle the ball more frequently than do group drills.

⟹ *Use group drills sparingly,* or in these instances: (a) when there are only one or two balls for the entire team, (b) where only one or two players at a time can shoot, (c) when you want to practice teamwork, or (d) when you want to slow down the pace. Group drills leave many players idle a majority of the time.

⟹ *Arrange your players so that everyone has room* to practice the same drill. We recommend the grid system for this purpose, but you may prefer another arrangement. Make sure there is ample space for all players to be active at once.

⟹ *Emphasize performance, not winning,* when your players compete in drills. Also be sure to match up players by skill and physical maturity to avoid lopsided drill competition.

What Soccer Drills Should I Use?

You now have all the skill and organizational information you need to conduct soccer drills that will prepare your players for regulation as well as small-sided and indoor soccer. Therefore, let's take a look at some drills that you can use to improve your players' individual offensive and defensive skills. We've identified each drill as being ideally suited for regulation soccer (RS), small-sided soccer (SSS), or indoor soccer (IS). Look for these abbreviations after each drill title.

Offensive Drills

Passing and Shooting

Name. Take a Walk (RS, SSS, IS)

Purpose. To learn accurate passing

Organization. Have players pair up and pass the ball to each other. Players walk along the field, passing the ball back and forth before gradually progressing to passing while jogging and running.

Coaching Points. Emphasize making quick passes and using proper receiving techniques. Also stress to players that they should pass the ball far enough ahead of a teammate moving forward.

Variations:

Pass Ahead. Partners pass ahead, leading players with the ball (see Figure 7.21).

Pass Through Cones or Legs. Partners pass through cones to each other or through each other's legs.

Pass and Shoot. Partners pass the ball to penalty arc and shoot at goal.

Name. Through the Cones (SSS)

Purpose. To work on accurate and correct passing technique

Organization. Divide players into two equal teams. Use cones to set off an area approximately 40 by 30 yards. Place goals at

■ **Figure 7.21** Pass Ahead Drill.

opposite ends (cones should be about 4 feet apart). Teams compete as in regular soccer, and a point is scored only when one
player successfully passes to a teammate through one of the
goals at either end of the field.

Coaching Points. Emphasize passing with either the side of the foot
or the instep. Toe-passes should not count for points. Also stress
the need for the players on each team to support their teammate
when he or she has the ball.

Name. Long Pass (RS, SSS)

Purpose. To work on correct technique for making long passes in
the air

Organization. Divide players into two equal teams. Use cones to
mark off an area approximately 40 by 30 yards and to create a
restricted zone in the middle of the playing area about 20 yards

long. Players work on making long passes to each other in the air, over the restricted zone. Defenders can be added to have players work on passing under pressure.

Coaching Points. Make sure that players kick the ball correctly, with the instep. The nonkicking foot should be placed slightly behind the ball while the kicking foot should strike the ball below center to make it rise.

Name. Pass and Move (RS, SSS, IS)

Purpose. To teach players to pass to players who are open and to move to an open area after passing

Organization. Divide the team into groups of four. Assign three players to pass the ball inside a grid with one defender trying to intercept.

Coaching Points. Have offensive players work on getting open rather then standing after passing the ball. Offensive players should attempt to maintain a triangle formation. Initially, tell defensive players to try to force passes and to move toward the passer to reduce the passing angle. After offensive players have learned to pass effectively, encourage more aggressive defensive play. Defenders can then try to anticipate and perhaps intercept the ball from the offense.

Name. Circle Passing (RS, SSS, IS)

Purpose. To emphasize accurate passing

Organization. Players form a circle and pass to each other (see Figure 7.22). Players can pass to any team member in the circle except to the players on either side of them.

Coaching Points. Passes should be crisp and accurate. Make players aware of passes that are inaccurate, too soft, or too hard. Use this drill only during the initial stages of learning, then move on to its variations to provide more of a challenge to players' skills.

Variations:

Pressure Passing. One player is in the middle of the circle and tries to intercept passes.

Pass Around. A player in the middle of the circle passes around the circle to each player.

■ **Figure 7.22** Circle Passing Drill.

Name. Roll and Shoot (RS, SSS, IS)

Purpose. To practice goalkeeping and shooting on goal

Organization. Line up three players on each side of the penalty area. Have another player on each side alternately roll or toss balls to the first player in line for shots on goals. Also station a player on each side of the goal to retrieve balls. Players should wait to pass the ball to shooters until the goalie reestablishes position. Have players rotate through all positions.

Coaching Points. Have players concentrate on shooting accurately by squaring up to the goal and following through on their kicks.

Name. Wall Pass (IS)

Purpose. To improve *indoor* passing technique and to learn to use the wall to team's advantage

Organization. Line players single file about 10 feet away from the wall surrounding indoor arena. Place a single cone 5 to 10 yards away from the first player in line. Player dribbles ball to cone and uses the wall to execute a wall pass around the cone. Having received the ball from the wall, player may shoot on goal (see Figure 7.23).

Coaching Points. Emphasis should be on correct passing technique.

■ **Figure 7.23** Wall Pass Drill.

Name. Shots Off the Board (IS)

Purpose. To improve *indoor* shooting technique and learn how to use indoor wall to advantage

Organization. Arrange players into two lines outside the penalty area and facing the goal. Players in one line dribble ball down the side of the court and pass the ball hard off the wall so that it will rebound to an area in front of goal where the other player can shoot on goal (see Figure 7.24). Players should learn to go down both the right and left sides.

Coaching Points. Get players to see the wall as a sixth player on the court. Players should use correct technique in passing as they learn to use the wall to "center" the ball for another player.

■ Figure 7.24　Shots Off the Board Drill.

Name. **In the Crease** (IS)

Purpose. To learn how to redirect ball with any part of the body (excluding hands) in front of an *indoor* goal

Organization. Position four or five players in or around the *crease*, the area immediately in front of the goal. Players learn to use their heads or any other part of their bodies, excluding hands and arms, to deflect balls passed or shot in the air or on the ground away from the goalie and into the goal.

Coaching Points. Remind players that there is no offside in indoor soccer, and thus they can stand in the crease as ball is advanced toward opponents' goal.

Trapping

Name. **Pass and Trap** (RS, SSS, IS)

Purpose. To practice various types of trapping

Organization. Have players pair up and toss or pass the ball to each other. The receiving player should trap the ball using a specified trap: foot, thigh, or chest (see Figure 7.25).

Coaching Points. Highlight moving to the ball; reaching out with the foot, leg, or chest to meet the ball; cushioning the ball; and keeping the ball close to the feet.

■ **Figure 7.25** Pass and Trap Drill.

Dribbling

Name. Wiggle Dribble (RS, SSS, IS)

Purpose. To teach players to look up while dribbling

Organization. Make sure each player has a ball. Have players gather inside a grid area and dribble, trying not to touch the other players or their balls. At first, make the grid area large enough so players have plenty of room to dribble. As players become more skilled, decrease the size of the grid area.

Coaching Points. Tell players to keep an eye on what's going on around them, even if they lose control of the ball at times.

Name. Whistle Dribble (RS, SSS, IS)

Purpose. To practice changing direction quickly

Organization. Use a whistle and point in the direction players are to dribble or use commands such as "Stop," "Forward," "Right," and "Left" (see Figure 7.26).

Coaching Points. Keep players guessing by varying your commands. Have players focus on keeping the ball close to their feet.

■ **Figure 7.26** Whistle Dribble Drill.

Name. Fake-Out (RS, SSS, IS)

Purpose. To improve dribbling skills

Organization. Pair up players and have them face one another. Give
  one player in each pair a ball, and have the partners of those players assume a defensive position. Tell the ballhandlers to fake with
  head, shoulders, hips, or feet and try to dribble past the player
  marking them.

Coaching Points. Advise offensive players to watch their opponents
  and look for a chance to take advantage. Also stress the importance of keeping the ball close to the feet. Defenders should be
  instructed to keep their eyes on the ball and not to get off balance
  because of a fake.

Heading

Name. Toss and Head (RS, SSS, IS)

Purpose. To get a feel for proper heading technique and to improve heading accuracy

Organization. First, have players hold a ball with both hands, bring it up near their foreheads, and then gently strike it while keeping their eyes open and mouths closed. Then ask players to pair up, and have one of the players toss the ball like a soft throw-in so the other player can head it (see Figure 7.27). Have players switch after 10 attempts.

■ **Figure 7.27**   Toss and Head Drill.

Coaching Points. Emphasize keeping the eyes open and moving forward to the ball. Remind players to keep their mouths closed as they head the ball to avoid injury. Watch that tossers are using correct throw-in technique, and that pairs get no more than 5 yards apart.

Variation:

Heading for Goal. Players head the tossed ball at the goal.

Name. Head to Head (SS)

Purpose. To improve ability to head under pressure in front of the goal

Organization. Divide players into two teams. Designate one group as "attackers" and the other group as "defenders." Two players (one from each group) go one-on-one as the coach tosses the ball in the air in front of the goal. The "attacker" heads the ball into the goal, while the "defender" tries to head the ball away from the goal.

Coaching Points. Stress the importance of positioning oneself under the ball before attempting to head the ball. Players should be encouraged to jump to head.

Name. Throw-Head-Catch (RS, SS)

Purpose. Players work on heading skills, heading under pressure, and heading for accuracy

Organization. Divide players into two teams. Scrimmage should occur in an area a little smaller than half a regulation field with regulation-size goals at each end. To advance the ball down the field, the member of one team must toss it to a teammate, who heads it to a third player, who can either head or catch the ball, and so on. The player carrying the ball may take three steps before tossing it to a teammate to head. Goals can be scored only on headers. When the ball touches the ground, it is turned over to the other team.

Coaching Points. The emphasis is upon learning to head correctly and accurately while under pressure. Point out the importance of supporting the teammate with the ball.

Name. Corner Kick (RS, SS)

Purpose. To learn to head to shoot on goal. This drill is a small-sided one, but it may be done on a regulation field as well.

Organization. Divide players into two groups and position them in front of the goal. Have a coach or a designated player take the corner kicks and place the ball in front of the goal mouth so players have the opportunity to head the ball into the goal (see Figure 7.28).

Coaching Points. Tell players to meet the ball in the air when they go to head. If they wait for the ball to hit them, they may find heading a bit painful.

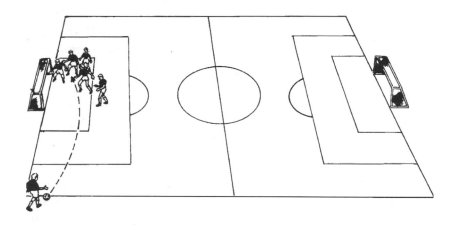

■ **Figure 7.28**   Corner Kick Drill.

Defensive Drills

Footwork

Name. Side Step and Crossover Practice (RS, SSS, IS)

Purpose. To practice moving sideways

Organization. Line up players facing you. Call out, "Side step" or "Crossover" as you point in the direction players are to move.

Coaching Points. Emphasize using the side step, or slide, to move short distances and the crossover to move longer distances.

Marking and Tackling

Name. Defensive One-on-One (RS, SSS, IS)

Purpose. To practice marking and tackling

Organization. Have players pair up. Designate one player to dribble for 30 yards and another to try to take the ball away. Players switch roles after the dribbler crosses the 30-yard mark.

Coaching Points. Begin with tackling from the front, and progress to tackling from the side. Watch that players tackle the ball rather than the person. Also, do not allow players to tackle from behind. Encourage offensive players to work on dribbling technique.

Name. Go-For-It (RS, SSS)

Purpose. To develop proper tackling and dribbling technique

Organization. Use cones to mark off an area of 20 by 20 yards and create small goals—cones 4 feet apart—at opposite ends. Divide players into two teams and have each team count off consecutively "one," "two," "three," and so on. Have teams line up at opposite ends of field, on both sides of their goal. The coach stands to the side of the playing area with a pool of balls and calls out the number of the first two players, who go one-on-one, each trying to score on his or her own goal. Each pair of players is given five balls to score on their own goal. Coaches can also call two or three numbers at a time.

Coaching Points. Coaches should emphasize correct dribbling and tackling techniques as well as the need to shoot at the first opportunity.

Name. Containment (RS, SSS)

Purpose. To work on containment, tackling, and dribbling techniques

Organization. Use cones to mark off an area approximately 10 by 5 yards. Divide players into two teams, attackers and defenders. Players go one-on-one, the attacker trying to dribble the ball past or around the defender and over the end line. Defenders attempt to contain attackers, that is, to stay goalside of attackers and force them to lose the ball by making a mistake. Play always starts with both players on their lines at ends of the playing area.

Coaching Points. Tell defenders to tackle for the ball only when they are fairly sure to win the ball. Otherwise, they should "contain" the attackers, forcing them to one side or the other, and out of the middle. Tell attackers to keep the ball close to their feet and frequently change speed and direction.

Name. Indoor Containment (IS)

Purpose. To work on containment, tackling, and dribbling techniques

Organization. This drill is very similar to the containment drill described previously. Attackers and defenders go one-on-one in a very restricted area. The attacker tries to dribble around the defender.

Coaching Points. Stress the need to contain the attacker instead of going for a tackle. In indoor soccer, a missed tackle near the goal often results in a scoring opportunity for the other team.

Name. Space Raiders (RS, SSS, IS)

Purpose. To improve dribbling, marking, and tackling skills

Organization. Choose two players to be "raiders." All other players are to dribble a ball inside the grid. Raiders do not have a ball, and they try to steal the other players' balls without fouling (see Figure 7.29). Players who lose balls become additional raiders and must help steal others' balls. The game ends when all players have lost their balls.

Coaching Points. Make this into a competitive group activity by dividing the players into small groups and comparing how many balls each group can steal in 60 seconds. Emphasize correct defensive footwork, position, and tackling techniques.

■ **Figure 7.29**   Space Raiders Drill.

Name. Crab Soccer (RS, SSS)

Purpose. To improve dribbling skills

Organization. Mark out an area approximately 5 by 5 yards and designate two players to assume the "crab" position. Make sure that each of the remaining players has a ball. Players dribble the ball in the restricted area while the crabs try to kick as many balls as possible out of the square (see Figure 7.30). Once a player's ball is kicked out, he or she becomes a crab. The last player with a ball is the winner.

Coaching Points. Tell dribblers to keep the ball close to their feet and to work on changing directions and changing speeds frequently. They should dribble the ball with the foot furthest away from the nearest crab.

■ **Figure 7.30**   Crab Soccer Drill.

Name. Mark-up Player-to-Player (RS, SSS, IS)

Purpose. To work on principles of defense, specifically marking and covering

Organization. Use the penalty area for this drill. Players compete four versus four or five versus five. The attackers attempt to score a goal while the defenders each take an attacker and work on "marking-up" player-to-player. The coach stands outside the penalty area with a pool of balls and feeds balls to the attacking team. After one team attacks for 5 or 10 minutes, players change roles, and defenders become the attackers and try to score. Goalkeeper is optional.

Coaching Points. Stress the need to mark-up the attacking team one-on-one. The player with the ball should be marked as well as his teammates without the ball. Attackers are encouraged to pass and move to space in order to elude defenders to set up for a shot on goal.

Goalkeeping

Name. Vacuum Cleaner (RS, SSS, IS)

Purpose. To teach proper goalkeeping technique

Organization. Have players practice goalkeeping by rolling balls to each other and scooping them up like a vacuum cleaner. Progress to kicking the ball and using faster speeds as players improve.

Coaching Points. Watch for players reaching out and lunging for the ball. Emphasize that they should move in front of the ball, bend down to meet the ball, scoop it up, and cradle it to their chests.

Name. Half-Moon Shoot (RS, SSS, IS)

Purpose. To practice good goalkeeping movement and handling of the ball

Organization. Assign a goalkeeper to each goal. Have five players line up in a semicircle in front of the goal (see Figure 7.31). Each player in the semicircle should have a ball and an assigned number. From the center circle call out numbers every 7 seconds until all five players on each end have shot. Repeat the drill and total up goals for each end. Give each player a chance at goalkeeping and have the goalies who allowed the fewest goals shoot on goal.

Coaching Points. Concentrate on good goalkeeping form. The goalie should move in front of the ball, and once the ball is caught, hold onto it tightly. Have shooters start out with soft, easy shots and gradually progress to full-speed shots. Be sure the goalie is ready before you call out the number of the next shooter.

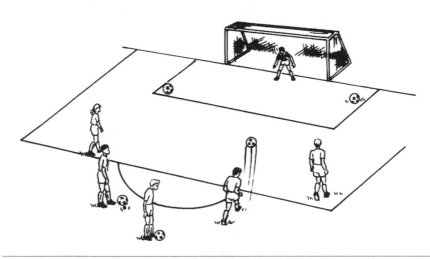

■ **Figure 7.31**   Half-Moon Shoot Drill.

Name. Three Goals Scrimmage (RS, SSS, IS)

Purpose. To develop goalie skills as well as principles of attacking and defending

Organization. For this drill, use an area not quite as large as half a regulation playing field. Arrange three cones in a triangle in the middle, making sure the cones are a goal's width apart. Designate one player as goalie. Divide the remaining players into two teams, which take turns attacking and defending. The team with the ball is always the attacking team while the other must defend. If the defending team wins the ball, it goes on attack, and the attackers become defenders. When goalies win the ball, they distribute it to one of the four corners to a player on the team that was defending.

Coaching Points. Encourage players to work on attacking and defending. The attackers must also pass the ball around in order to get a good opportunity on goal. The players defending should try to mark up player-to-player. Also, this drill gives the goalie an excellent workout.

Variation:

Two Goals Scrimmage. This drill is conducted the same as the one previously described, except that two cones are placed a goal's width apart in the middle of the field.

How Do I Get My Players to Play as a Team?

It's very important to emphasize development of individual skills when coaching young athletes. However, youngsters who participate in soccer games must know how to work as part of a team. Therefore, you must be prepared to teach players basic offensive and defensive team principles.

The most effective method of teaching these principles to young players is through small-sided games. Small-sided games allow the coach to emphasize one or more principles of offense and defense. Of the small-sided games described in this chapter, "Six-on-Four," "Four-on-Four Plus Two," and "Throw-In Scrimmage" are useful in teaching attacking and defending tactics in preparation for regulation soccer. Drills more suited for small-sided and indoor soccer are "Four-on-Two," "Four Goals Scrimmage," and "Shoot the Moving Ball." Of course, these drills are interchangeable: "Four-on-Two" can be used to teach players to defend when outnumbered by attackers in a regulation game, and "Four-on-Four Plus Two" may be used for indoor or small-sided soccer.

What About Team Offense?

In soccer, a team's offense is designed to do two things. The offensive team's primary objective is to move the ball downfield and score. A secondary goal is to maintain ball possession so the opposing team cannot score. The following tactics will help your team accomplish these goals.

The Triangle Method

Essential to any soccer team's success is how players support their teammates on the field. Teaching the triangle concept is one way to reinforce the need to spread out, provide support, and provide the dribbler with more options. Simply put, this method involves the creation of a triangle formation on the field, with the dribbler generally at the apex (see Figure 8.1).

A   C

B ● ◄ Ball

■ **Figure 8.1**   The triangle method.

By maintaining a triangle, players *A*, *B*, and *C* will be able to spread out the defense and at the same time provide player *B* with more options.

The triangle formation is used in many sports, such as hockey, lacrosse, and basketball, where a fluid, dynamic interplay is required. To teach young players proper triangle positioning, you should use the easiest possible explanation. One method is to position players along the outer edges of the dribbler's field of vision. Players can find these outer edges by swinging both arms from behind the back around to the front until they are just visible.

Move With and Without the Ball

Offensive players are easy to mark if they are inactive. Encourage your players to move continually to an open area to receive passes. If teammates are not open, the dribbler should move the ball to an open area. This tactic will put pressure on the defense and probably cause one of the defensive players to leave his or her player, leaving one offensive player open for a pass. When a pass is made, the player to whom the pass was intended should come to meet the ball.

Error Detection and Correction for Receiving Passes

Passing takes teamwork. Often, what are considered bad passes are, in fact, good passes that were improperly received. Therefore, don't simply conclude that the passer was at fault; a stolen pass may also result from an exceptional defensive play or poor receiving technique.

ERROR: Receiver waiting for a pass to arrive when a defender is in the area

CORRECTION

1. Tell players to be aware of the pass, including its direction and velocity.

2. Instruct players to notice the position of defenders in relation to the path of the pass.

3. Insist that receivers move to meet the ball as quickly as possible (see Figure 8.2) while still maintaining sufficient control to trap the pass.

■ **Figure 8.2** Receiver moving to meet the ball.

Spread Out the Attack

Have your players keep distance between each other on the field. By spreading your offensive attack, your team will open up space for dribbling, passing, and scoring opportunities. Bunching together brings more defenders into position to intercept a pass or steal the ball. Also, when offensive players are too close together, more than one player can be guarded by only one defender.

Error Detection and Correction for Offensive Attack

Young players have a hard time understanding offensive strategies. However, there is one soccer team concept that kids can learn: Attack with width and depth. With this tactic offensive players spread out across the field in a zigzag pattern. Then players closer to the goal can receive penetrating passes, and their teammates behind them can serve as safety valves for passes or as midfielders to prevent opposing players from taking steals unchallenged downfield for a goal.

ERROR: Offensive players positioned in a straight line across the field (see Figure 8.3)

CORRECTION

1. Get depth to the attack by having your players form two big "V"s on the offensive end of the field (see Figure 8.4).
2. Tell players to be aware of their positions relative to offensive teammates and try to form triangles across the field.

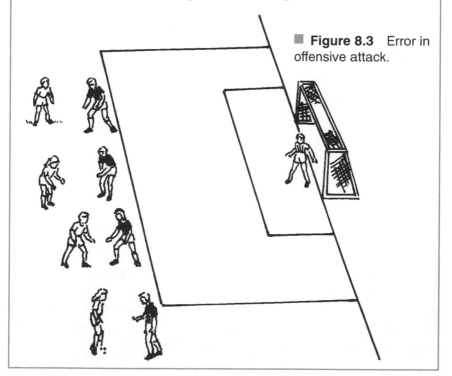

■ **Figure 8.3**   Error in offensive attack.

(continued)

Error Detection and Correction (*continued*)

■ **Figure 8.4** Correct offensive attack.

Pass and Shoot Often

Quick, frequent passes require the defense to adjust constantly. Also, when defenders are out of position, it is easier to shoot the ball to the goal. The more shots on goal taken by your players, the greater your team's chances to score, but make sure they're good shots from reasonable distances and angles.

Center the Ball

Your players will have more room to pass and dribble if they bring the ball down the side of the field. Defenders tend to bunch up in the center of the field, but if the defense spreads out and attempts to cover the sides of the field, it should open up the middle.

Once the ball is near the goal, your players should look to get the ball to a teammate in the center of the field. A centered ball to an offensive player in front of the goal puts a great amount of pressure on the defenders because the offense can attack from either side or the center. Shooters also have the best angle at the goal from the center of the field, as illustrated in Figure 8.5.

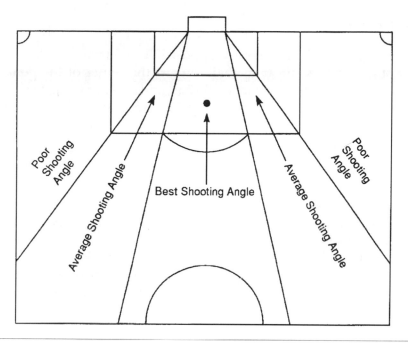

■ **Figure 8.5** Ratings of shooting angles in soccer.

Prepare for Special Situations

Several instances during a soccer game require special offensive attacks. The following situations arise when the ball goes out-of-bounds or when a foul is called:

Throw-Ins

The throw-in and corner kick situations represent good opportunities to run set plays. Remind your players to be careful when they throw the ball in, particularly when near the opponent's goal. The primary objective in that situation is to play it safe and maintain possession. When players throw the ball in on your team's offensive end, however, they should look for an open teammate in the best position to score or begin the offensive attack. Remember, the offside rule is waived for throw-ins. So encourage your players to charge the goal area if they see an opening in the defense.

Corner Kicks

Corner kicks are good scoring opportunities. Have the player attempting the kick direct the ball toward the center of the penalty box. Teammates should react to the ball and attempt to get free for a quick shot on goal. Again, a set play that brings the ball close to the goal and creates a player advantage is recommended.

Goal Kicks

A goal kick, taken from inside the goal area, may be a short pass to a teammate to initiate the offense and keep it away from the defense or a long one to clear it from your team's defensive end and, perhaps, start a quick offensive attack. The type of goal kick desired will depend on the game situation, but in all cases the ball must clear the penalty area before being touched by another player.

Free Kicks

Free kicks represent great scoring opportunities. Indirect and direct free kicks should be executed with set plays. Ask experienced soccer coaches or consult more in-depth soccer books for some ideas. Teach your team to take free kicks as quickly as possible, before the defense can set up. Defensive players must give the offense room to put the ball into play. Make sure your players know that the ball must be touched by more than one player on indirect free kicks.

What About Team Defense?

Playing good defense involves using correct technique and working together with teammates. Certainly, individual steals and blocks of the ball are exciting, but they are much more likely to happen with good defensive *teamwork*. The following tactics will help your team become a strong defensive unit.

Reduce the Passing and Shooting Angle

A good defensive tactic to teach your players is to get close to the player with the ball. The closer your defenders are to the player with the ball, the more difficult it is for that player to pass and shoot. Thus, your players will have a better chance of stealing or blocking the ball when the opponent passes or shoots. Remind your players that they must first be between the opponent with the ball and the goal to reduce the shooting angle (see Figure 8.6).

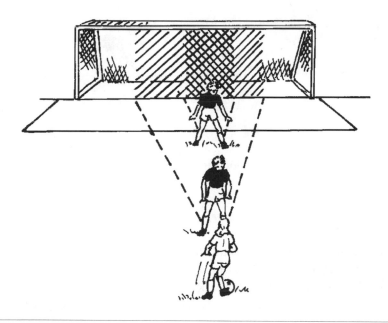

■ **Figure 8.6**   Defender moving up to reduce the shooting angle.

Kick the Ball to the Outside

If the opposing team is able to keep the ball in the center of the field on its offensive end, it will have a better shooting angle, and your defense will have a difficult time preventing goals. Therefore, instruct your defenders to kick the ball to the side of the field when the other team gets the ball close to the goal (see Figure 8.7). Your goalkeeper will appreciate it!

■ **Figure 8.7**   Defense clearing the ball.

Kick the Ball to the Goalkeeper

A good way to protect the goal is to pass the ball to your goalkeeper. Note that a FIFA (Fédération Internationale de Football Associations) rule prohibits the goalie from picking up the ball if it has been intentionally passed back to the goalie by a field player. The goalie may use the feet to handle such a pass. The ball should be passed to the sides of the goal, not in front of it. Warn your players to look for opponents sneaking to steal passes they intended for the goalie. Remind goalkeepers to come out of the goal to meet the ball and to call for the ball if they want it.

Error Detection and Correction for Positioning on Defense

Players not guarding the dribbler often make the mistake of positioning themselves directly between the goal and a teammate guarding the dribbler. Teach your players to position themselves at an angle from their teammate guarding the dribbler; they'll cover a wider area and severely limit the passing and shooting options of the dribbler.

ERROR:　Defending from a position directly behind a teammate, as in Figure 8.8

■ **Figure 8.8**　Error in marking away from the ball.

(continued)

Error Detection and Correction (continued)

CORRECTION

1. Tell players to know where the ball is at all times.

2. Have them note the position of their teammate guarding the dribbler.

3. Have them note their own positions in relation to the opponent's goal.

4. Advise them to assume positions at angles from the straight line between their teammate guarding the dribbler and the goal (see Figure 8.9).

■ **Figure 8.9** Correct marking away from the ball.

Offensive Team Drills

Name. Triangle Passing (RS, SSS, IS)

Purpose. To practice moving the ball downfield and maintain triangle formation

Organization. Have players form three lines, 5 to 7 yards apart. The first player in each of the outside lines should sprint 5 yards straight downfield and be ready to receive a pass from the first player in the middle line. The three players should maintain this triangle formation while passing the ball to each other as they walk, jog, or run down the field. Passes can be one touch or two. Players always have two passing options. Allow the first trio to move down the field 15 yards before the next group begins. As your team improves, add defenders who try to steal the ball.

Coaching Points. Tell players to look downfield and to be aware of the ball and other players. Emphasize controlling the ball with one touch, then passing.

Variation:

Triangle Passing With Defender. A good game to reinforce the triangle and make it more challenging is to introduce a defender. First, as shown in Figure 8.10, form a 20 by 20 foot square.

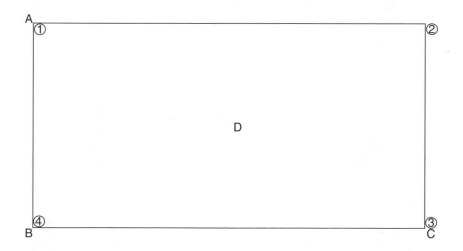

■ **Figure 8.10**   Triangle Passing With Defender Drill.

Players *A*, *B*, and *C* pass to one another, always maintaining a triangle. To provide proper support, players need to move around continuously. For example, if *B* passes to *C*, *A* will have to run to position 2 to complete a triangle with *C* at its center. If *B* passes to *A*, *C* has to occupy position 2 to complete the triangle for *A*. *D* is the defender and tries to intercept the pass. If successful, *D* switches with the player whose pass was intercepted.

Name. Give-and-Go (RS, SSS, IS)

Purpose. To work on gaining an advantage on the defense and improving passing and shooting skills

Organization. Have players get into groups of four. Position two offensive players 20 to 30 yards in front of the goal. Designate a player to be goalie and another to serve as defender. Have the defender confront the offensive player with the ball. The offensive player should pass it to the teammate, whom the defender will seek to cover. If the defender gains position on the offensive player receiving the pass, that offensive player should make a return pass to the teammate (see Figure 8.11), who should attempt to shoot the ball past the goalie.

Coaching Points. Emphasize teamwork between the offensive players, with special concern for the timing and accuracy of passes. Stress the importance of scoring to complete the play.

■ **Figure 8.11** Give-and-Go Drill.

Name. Throw-In Step-Out (RS, SSS)

Purpose. To practice proper throw-in technique

Organization. Ask players to pair up, and have them practice throw-ins to each other at a distance of 15 feet. Instruct the throwing player to take one step back each time the ball is properly thrown and controlled.

Coaching Points. Insist on correct technique: starting behind the head, throwing with both hands, and keeping both feet on the ground. Remind receiving players to trap the ball without using their hands.

Defensive Team Drills

Name. Glue Person (RS, SSS)

Purpose. To practice defensive and offensive movement

Organization. Tell two offensive players to get open for a throw-in or a pass from a passer. Instruct two defensive players to mark their assigned offensive player as closely as possible—looking to steal the ball only if they have a good chance of being successful.

Coaching Points. Emphasize that the defensive players should stay between the offensive players they are marking and the goal. Remind offensive players to pass to the open space, not directly to their partners.

Name. Cut Down the Angle (RS, SSS, IS)

Purpose. To teach players the importance of reducing the passing angle

Organization. Two offensive players and one defensive player are inside a grid approximately 10 by 10 yards. The offensive player tries to pass against the defender. The defender guards the player without the ball until "Ball!" is called. Then the defender reduces the passing angle by positioning between the two offensive players and tries to intercept the ball (see Figure 8.12).

Coaching Points. Stress the need for the defensive player to stay between the offensive players.

■ **Figure 8.12** Cut Down the Angle Drill.

What Is a Good Way to Scrimmage?

Small-sided scrimmage formats, for example three-on-three or four-on-four on a reduced field (see Figure 8.13), give everyone a chance to handle the ball and participate. These are especially important learning opportunities for less skilled or less experienced players if the defensive pressure applied is not too great. Also, because fewer players are involved, these types of scrimmages allow for more contact with the ball and perhaps more rapid improvement.

You can also organize different types of minigames, such as games in which no dribbling is permitted. These activities force players to concentrate on certain skills, such as passing.

Full-fielded games, with the league-standard number of players per team, are fine—in fact, they are essential in preparing players for contests—but avoid using them each practice. There are many alternative activities that will allow your players to compete and that still permit maximum participation and involvement. Begin-

■ Figure 8.13　Small-sided scrimmage.

ners often benefit from six versus five and five versus four scrimmages that give the offensive team an edge. You can ensure success by participating as a player who plays offense for both teams. The following modified games are a sample of other scrimmage ideas you might use.

Name.　Soccer Baseball (RS)

Purpose.　To practice long kicks and passing

Organization.　Arrange a field with home plate, bases, and out-of-bounds lines. Divide players into teams of even ability and "play ball." Have "pitchers" pass the ball to "batters" with their feet. Batters kick the ball and attempt to reach first base before being touched by the ball, before the ball reaches the base, or before the ball is passed back to the pitcher. Batters who successfully reach first base can continue around the bases just as in baseball. Base runners are out if they get touched with the ball or if a fielder has control of the ball (with the feet) and tags the runner.

Coaching Points. Keep the game moving and the players interested in the game by not keeping track of outs. Have each team "bat" until each player has kicked.

Name. **Pass Through Zones** (RS, SSS, IS)

Purpose. To practice offensive movement, marking, and reducing passing angles

Organization. Divide the team into three teams, each with two players, and assign each to a 10-by-10-yard zone grid. Designate the two teams on the outside grids as the offensive teams and the team in the middle grid as the defensive team. Instruct offensive players to pass the ball constantly and accurately to either a teammate in the same zone or through the defensive zone to one of their teammates in the other zone (see Figure 8.14). Have the defensive unit switch to offense after stealing three passes. Give each team a turn to play defense.

■ **Figure 8.14** Pass Through Zones Drill.

Coaching Points. For offensive players, emphasize passing accurately and quickly to an open space. Encourage defensive players to stay between the players they are covering.

Name. Six-on-Four (RS, SSS, IS)

Purpose. To work on principles of offense and defense

Organization. This game is played in front of the goal and should include a goalie. Six attackers play against four defenders and try to score as often as they can. Defenders can score on an open goal placed near the halfway point of a regulation field.

Coaching Points. Attackers should be encouraged to work the ball down the wings and cross to the center as well as to pass the ball back to a supporting player. Because they are outnumbered, defenders learn to go two-on-one, at times even three-on-one. Defenders should try to force the attack out of the middle and must learn to cover for each other.

Name. Four-on-Four Plus Two (RS, SSS, IS)

Purpose. To work on principles of offense and defense, specifically upon taking advantage of numerical superiority on attack and learning to defend when outnumbered

Organization. This game should be played on a field approximately one quarter the size of a normal playing field. Small goals are placed at opposite ends of the playing field. The two free players are always on the attacking team.

Coaching Points. Emphasis should be placed on creating numerical superiority on attack as well as upon learning to defend when outnumbered. Tell players that, when they are defending, they should not lunge at the ball with their tackling foot; such a move will likely throw the defender off balance, making it easy for his opponent to beat him.

Name. Four Goals Scrimmage (RS, SSS)

Purpose. To work on principles of attack, specifically spreading out

Organization. Players are divided into two teams and play a regular scrimmage on half a regulation field. Each team, however, has two goals to defend instead of one (see Figure 8.15).

Coaching Points. Emphasis is upon being creative while attacking, drawing the players from the other team to defend on one goal and then "changing fields"—that is, switching the play *across* the field—to attack on the other goal. The only goals that count are those that are below the level of the waist.

■ **Figure 8.15**   Four Goals Scrimmage Drill.

Name. Throw-In Scrimmage (RS, SSS)

Purpose. To work on generating attack upon a throw-in

Organization. Use cones to mark off an area approximately 40 by 30 yards with goals at each end. Goalies may be used for this small-sided scrimmage. Divide players into two teams. Teams take turns attacking. Each team gets five consecutive throw-ins.

Coaching Points. Coaches need to emphasize correct throw-in technique. They should also emphasize that the player receiving the ball must "show"—or move to open space—to receive the throw-in.

Name. Shoot the Moving Ball

Purpose. To work on shooting under pressure

Organization. This one-on-one drill has many variations. Have players get into two lines—attackers and defenders—about twenty yards out from the goal. A defender passes the ball to open space in front of attacker, who runs on the ball to shoot while defender pursues and puts attacker under pressure (see Figure 8.16).

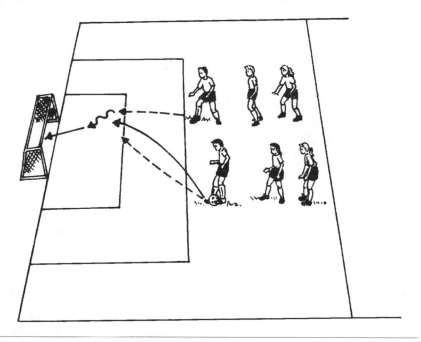

■ **Figure 8.16** Shoot the Moving Ball Drill.

Coaching Points. Tell the defender not to take the ball from the attacker but to put pressure on the attacker running on and shooting the ball. Emphasize correct shooting technique.

Variation:

On a signal from the coach, two players from each group enter the penalty area. The coach feeds five consecutive balls to the attacking team, who must try to score. If defenders win the ball, they become attackers.

Name. Four-on-Two (RS, SSS, IS)

Purpose. To work on defending while outnumbered

Organization. Divide players into attackers and defenders. Attackers begin just outside the penalty area while defenders are grouped behind the goal. Four attackers go against two defenders and try to score on the goalie.

Coaching Points. Tell the attackers to pass the ball around—out to the wing, back to a supporting midfielder, and so on—in order to draw defenders out of position and create a scoring opportunity. Tell defenders not to play "square," or in a straight line. One defender always pressures the ball carrier while the other covers for him. If one defender is beaten, the covering defender takes his place and the beaten defender then moves back to provide cover.

How Can I Learn More About Coaching and Soccer?

Successful coaches develop from several years of hard work, making mistakes, and learning new coaching methods. And the best coaches continue to seek more information. Here are three ways you can learn more about coaching and soccer:

➡ *Keep coming back.* Your players improve when they have fun, are informed, and are motivated to get better. You will too!

➡ *Attend coaching clinics.* We recommend the Leader Level Course that is offered throughout the country by the American Sport Education Program (ASEP).

➡ *Read up on soccer and coaching.* ASEP offers an excellent source for more soccer information in *Coaching Soccer Effectively*, by Christopher A. Hopper and Michael S. Davis. And an excellent, general coaching resource provided by ASEP is *Successful Coaching*.

The American Sport Education Program would be happy to help you further your coaching knowledge. For information or to order materials, contact us at

P.O. Box 5076
Champaign, IL 61825-5076
1-800-747-5698

Appendix A

Sample Season Plan for Beginning Soccer Players

Goal: To help players learn and practice the individual skills and team tactics needed to play a regulation game of soccer successfully.

T(10): Teach and practice the skill initially for 10 minutes
P(10): Review and practice the skill for 10 minutes
▲ These skills are practiced during drills

Skills	Week 1		Week 2		Week 3		Week 4		Time in Minutes
	Day 1	Day 2	Day 1	Day 2	Day 1	Day 2	Day 1	Day 2	
Warm-Up Exercises	T(5)	P(5)	P(5)	P(5)	P(5)	P(5)	P(5)	P(5)	40
Cool-Down Exercises	T(5)	P(5)	P(5)	P(5)	P(5)	P(5)	P(5)	P(5)	40
Passing									
Short	T(10)		▲	▲		▲	▲	▲	10
Long				T(10)					10
Drills	P(30)	P(20)		P(10)	P(10)			P(10)	60
Trapping									
Cushion		T(10)		▲		▲		▲	10
Drills		P(20)				P(10)		P(10)	40

								Total
Dribbling								
Ball Control	T(10)							10
Against opponents	T(10)					▲	▲	10
Drills		P(30)					P(10)	40
Heading								
Forward			T(10)			▲		10
Drills				P(10)			P(10)	20
Scoring								
Shooting		T(10)		▲	▲		▲	10
Drills			P(10)			P(10)		20
Goalkeeping								
Positioning					T(10)			10
Agility						T(10)		10
Handling							T(10)	10
Drills						P(10)	P(10)	20
Game Play								
Positions		T(10)						10
Full game		T(10) P(10)	P(20)	P(10)	P(20)	P(20)	P(20)	100
Small-sided scrimmages				P(20)	P(20)	P(10)	P(10)	60
Elapsed time	60	70	70	70	70	70	70	

Appendix B

Soccer Officiating Signals

Referee Signals

Advantage/Play on

Penalty kick
(points to penalty area)

Direct free kick

Indirect free kick

Goal kick

Corner kick

Caution or expulsion

Linesman Signals

Substitution

Throw-in

Corner kick

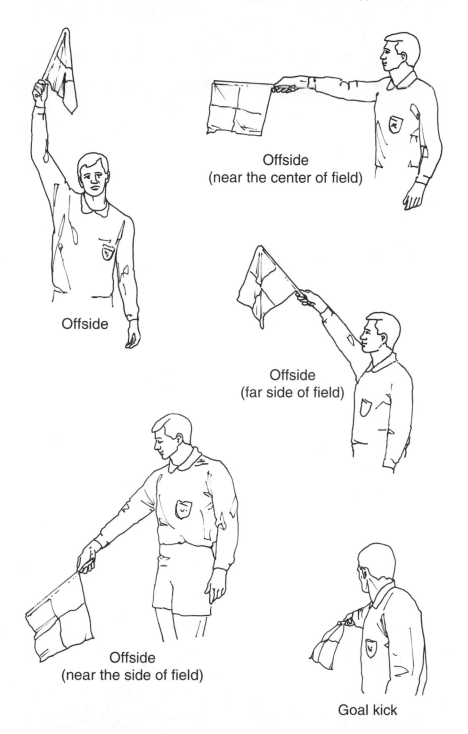

Offside

Offside
(near the center of field)

Offside
(far side of field)

Offside
(near the side of field)

Goal kick

Appendix C

Organizations to Contact for Coaching Children With Disabilities

American Athletic Association of the Deaf
3607 Washington Boulevard, Suite 4
Ogden, UT 84403-1737
(801) 393-8710
TTY: (801) 393-7916
Fax: (801) 393-2263

Disabled Sports USA
451 Hungerford Drive, Suite 100
Rockville, MD 20850
(301) 217-0960

Paralyzed Veterans of America
801 18th Street NW
Washington, DC 20006
(202) 872-1300
(800) 424-8200

Special Olympics International
1325 G Street NW, Suite 500
Washington, DC 20005
(202) 628-3630

U.S. Association of Blind Athletes
33 North Institute
Colorado Springs, CO 80903
(719) 630-0422

U.S. Cerebral Palsy Athletic Association
3810 West NW Highway, Suite 205
Dallas, TX 75220
(214) 351-1510

U.S. Les Autres Sports Association
1475 West Gray, Suite166
Houston, TX 77019-4926
(713) 521-3737

*S*occer books for coaches and players

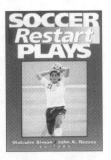

Soccer Restart Plays

J. Malcolm Simon, MA, and John A. Reeves, EdD, Editors

Foreword by Cliff McCrath

1994 • Paper • 152 pp • Item PSIM0521
ISBN 0-87322-521-X • $12.95 ($17.95 Canadian)

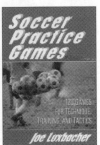

Soccer Practice Games

Joe Luxbacher

1995 • Paper • 152 pp • Item PLUX0554
ISBN 0-87322-554-6 • $13.95 ($19.95 Canadian)

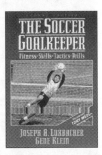

The Soccer Goalkeeper

(Second Edition)

**Joseph A. Luxbacher, PhD, and
Gene Klein, MEd**

Foreword by Tony Meola

1993 • Paper • 176 pp • Item PLUX0397
ISBN 0-87322-397-7 • $14.95 ($21.95 Canadian)

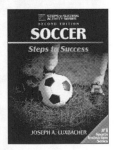

Soccer

Steps to Success

(Second Edition)

Joseph A. Luxbacher, PhD

1995 • Paper • 168 pp • Item PLUX0763
ISBN 0-87322-763-8 • $14.95 ($21.95 Canadian)

Prices are subject to change.

To place your order, U.S. customers **call
TOLL FREE 1 800 747-4457**. Customers
outside the U.S. place your order using the
appropriate telephone number/address
shown in the front of this book.

Human Kinetics
The Premier Publisher for Sports & Fitness

2335

ASEP Volunteer Level

The American Sport Education Program (ASEP) offers three Volunteer Level curriculums for adults who work with youth sport:

■ SportCoach ■ SportParent ■ SportDirector

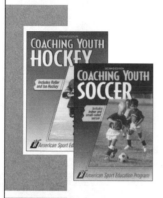

SportCoach

ASEP's SportCoach Program consists of two courses:

The **Rookie Coaches Course** provides inexperienced coaches with essential information for teaching the skills and strategies of a sport, including sample practice plans. Companion coaching guides are available for baseball, basketball, football, gymnastics, hockey, ski racing, softball, soccer, swimming, tennis, volleyball, and wrestling.

The **Coaching Young Athletes Course** is for second-year coaches and others who want more instruction in the principles of coaching than is offered in the Rookie Course.

SportParent

ASEP's SportParent Course is a 1- to 2-hour program that provides youth sport administrators and coaches with a practical and effective way to educate parents about their children's participation in sports.

The SportParent Course Package includes the *SportParent Facilitator Manual,* the *SportParent Video,* the *SportParent Survival Guide,* and the *SportParent* book.

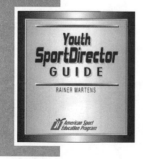

SportDirector

ASEP's SportDirector Program offers outstanding opportunities for youth sport directors to improve sport programs for the children in their community. The program includes a very practical *Youth SportDirector Guide* and a dynamic workshop.

American Sport Education Program
P.O. Box 5076
Champaign, IL 61825-5076
Fax: 217 351-1549

For more information on ASEP's Volunteer Level programs, call Toll-Free 1 800 747-5698.